God,
Help Me
Overcome My
Circumstances

MICHAEL YOUSSEF

D0008737

HARVEST HOUSE PUBLISHERS
EUGENE, OREGON

Unless otherwise indicated, all Scripture quotations are from The ESV® Bible (The Holy Bible, English Standard Version®), copyright © 2001 by Crossway, a publishing ministry of Good News Publishers. Used by permission. All rights reserved.

Verses marked KJV are from the King James Version of the Bible.

Cover by Knail, Salem, Oregon

Cover photo © Image Source Photography / Veer

Published in association with the literary agency of Wolgemuth & Associates, Inc.

GOD, HELP ME OVERCOME MY CIRCUMSTANCES

Copyright © 2015 by Michael Youssef
Published by Harvest House Publishers
Eugene, Oregon 97402
www.harvesthousepublishers.com

Library of Congress Cataloging-in-Publication Data
Youssef, Michael.
God, help me overcome my circumstances / Michael Youssef.
pages cm
ISBN 978-0-7369-5503-4 (pbk.)
ISBN 978-0-7369-5504-1 (eBook)
1. Resilience (Personality trait)—Religious aspects—Christianity. 2. Adjustment (Psychology)—Religious aspects—Christianity. 3. Life change events—Religious aspects—Christianity. 4. Success—Religious aspects—Christianity. 5. Hope—Religious aspects—Christianity. 6. Bible. Judges. I. Title.
BV4908.5.Y69 2015
248.4—dc23
                                                                    2014042877

All rights reserved. No part of this publication may be reproduced, stored in a retrieval system, or transmitted in any form or by any means—electronic, mechanical, digital, photocopy, recording, or any other—except for brief quotations in printed reviews, without the prior permission of the publisher.

Printed in the United States of America

15 16 17 18 19 20 21 22 23 / VP-JH / 10 9 8 7 6 5 4 3 2 1

To Barry Teague
in deep appreciation for a heart
that beats for Christ and his work
and a life that is dedicated to
blessing Jesus' kingdom.

Acknowledgments

I am grateful to Jim Denney and Don Gates for using their gifts to help make this book more relevant and practical.

Special thanks to the entire team at Harvest House Publishers—and especially to Bob Hawkins Jr., LaRae Weikert, and Rod Morris, who shared my dream and helped to enlarge the vision of this book.

Finally, thanks to the people of The Church of The Apostles in Atlanta, Georgia, for their constant encouragement and support. They were the first audience for this message, and they helped me to refine the message with their questions and helpful comments.

Contents

Introduction

These Stories Are About *Us*

The day after Christmas 2012, a cable television host interviewed a prominent pastor on his show. "You and I know," the host said, "that the Bible is, in many places, a flawed document...It's time for an amendment to the Bible. You should compile a new Bible."

This TV host expressed the spirit of the age in which we live. Mere human beings claim the right to edit and amend God's Word. They believe the Bible must change in order to accommodate the latest social fad or political cause. In this way, our culture mirrors the culture of Israel in the time of the Judges, when (as we read in Judges 17:6 and 21:25), "Everyone did what was right in his own eyes."

In our culture, and even in some parts of the church, God's Word is neglected and disrespected. If we don't like what the Bible says about sin, morality, the sanctity of the family, the sanctity of life, or the claim of Jesus to be the only way to God the Father, we just edit those parts out. We pretend that God didn't really say that, or he didn't really mean that. Forsaking the Bible, we simply do whatever is right in our own eyes.

The parallels between the book of Judges and our own post-Christian age are unmistakable—and many of these parallels are deeply troubling. If God did not allow the people of Israel to get away with their apostasy, why do we expect God to simply wink at our spiritual and moral defection? Has God changed? Out of his great love for Israel, God disciplined Israel and called the people to repentance again and again. So we have to ask ourselves, "Is God, out of his great love, disciplining our nation? And is he disciplining and refining the church?"

Again and again in the book of Judges, Israel strayed from God. And each time, God used enemy nations to oppress and discipline Israel and call the people to repentance. Today, as our nation faces decline, economic upheaval, global tensions, and the constant menace of terrorism, we have to ask ourselves: Is God using these circumstances to discipline us, to call us collectively and individually to repentance?

Whenever Israel repented and turned back to God, he sent a deliverer to rescue the people from their oppressors. The people God used as "judges," as deliverers of Israel, were not super-saints. As we will see, they were ordinary people with flaws and struggles and weaknesses, just like you and me. Don't ever think that God cannot use you. If God can use flawed human beings like Gideon and Samson, he can use you.

Another parallel we see between the time of the judges and the times in which we live is the abandonment of absolute truth. The moral relativism practiced in apostate Israel is no different from the moral relativism we see in our culture—and, tragically, in many of our churches—today. Both then and now, people rejected God's absolute standard of truth, and everyone did what was right in their own eyes. The nineteenth-century writer James Russell Lowell put it this way in a poem of protest and outrage against the vile practice of human slavery, a poem called "The Present Crisis" (1844):

> Truth forever on the scaffold,
>   Wrong forever on the throne,—
> Yet that scaffold sways the future,
>   and, behind the dim unknown,
> Standeth God within the shadow,
>   keeping watch above his own.

Truth was murdered on the scaffold in the time of the judges. Truth was murdered on the scaffold in James Russell Lowell's time. Truth is still on the scaffold today, in the twenty-first century. Wrong is still on the throne of the systems of this world. Yet God is keeping watch today, as he was back then.

In the pages that follow, you will see parallel after parallel between those times and our time. You will see that the stories in the book of Judges are not just Sunday school stories. They are stories about *our* time, *our* culture, *our* churches, *our* sins. They are stories about *us*.

And there is one more parallel between then and now. It's a parallel of hope and encouragement. In Judges 21:25, God's Word tells us *why* everyone did what was right in their own eyes. It was because, "In those days there was no king in Israel."

The people of Israel during that time had no authority figure to rule them, guide them, and hold them accountable. Israel had no king—but a king was coming.

At the close of the time of the judges, God appointed a prophet named Samuel who would anoint Israel's greatest king—a king named David. King David would become, in many ways, a symbolic foreshadowing of King Jesus.

David stood alone against a seemingly invincible enemy, Goliath, who mocked God and threatened God's people. David served as the representative of all the people. He killed Goliath and delivered the people of Israel. He was later crowned king and ruled all of Israel from his capital city, Jerusalem.

In much the same way, Jesus stood alone against Satan, who mocked God and threatened God's people. Jesus represented the entire human race when he hung upon the cross. Jesus destroyed Satan and delivered us from sin and death. He is coming again to be crowned King and to rule over all the earth from Jerusalem.

The nation of Israel was in moral and spiritual decline, and could not defend itself against its enemies. The people had no king, so everyone did what was right in his own eyes. Our own circumstances seem equally hopeless. Our nation, our world, and even our church are in moral and spiritual decline. We are under attack, we are in disarray, and everyone does what is right in his own eyes. But today, as in the time of the judges, our King is coming. When Jesus returns, he will rule with righteousness and justice.

Today, we cry out to the Lord, "God, help me overcome my circumstances!" Some of those circumstances may be the result of our own moral failure and spiritual defection. Have we, like ancient Israel, forgotten God's love for us? Have we forgotten all of his grace and goodness toward us in the past? Perhaps God is using these difficult circumstances to remind us how much we need him. Perhaps God is calling us to repentance.

I hope that in the pages of the book of Judges, we will see God's love for us, and that our love for him would be rekindled. As we pray, "God, help me overcome my circumstances," may we also pray, "God, I repent of my sin. I recommit myself to you. I choose to live for you. Come be the Lord of my life once more!"

No matter how dark and troubled our circumstances, God

stands ready to deliver us. Even though Truth is on the scaffold and Wrong is on the throne, our King is coming. He will come in victory. He will deliver us. He will save us.

So turn the page. Let's explore this ancient book and hear God's message for us today.

1

Tales of Defection
and Deliverance

The book of Judges is one of the most dramatic books of the Bible. It could spin off dozens of epic adventure movies, political intrigue and spy novels, and even soap operas. On the surface, its tales provide fascinating, even thrilling reading.

But on a deeper level, this book is a powerful indictment of the condition I call "spiritual amnesia." Again and again throughout Judges, we see the people of Israel forgetting God's love, God's commands, and God's Word. The people experience God's blessing, they become self-satisfied and prideful, and they descend into spiritual defection and defeat. Then and only then do they remember God and cry out to him for deliverance. Then God graciously sends a deliverer.

The contrast between Joshua and Judges is stark. While Joshua was an account of Israel's victories in its conquest of the Promised

Land, Judges is the account of Israel's failure and defeat. Here is an outline of the book of Judges:

1. Israel fails to completely conquer the Promised Land— Judges 1:1–3:4

2. The judge Othniel—Judges 3:7-11

3. The judge Ehud—Judges 3:12-30

4. The judge Shamgar—Judges 3:31

5. The judge Deborah—Judges 4–5

6. The judge Gideon—Judges 6:1–8:35

7. The judge Abimelech—Judges 9

8. The judge Tola—Judges 10:1-2

9. The judge Jair—Judges 10:3-5

10. The judge Jephthah—Judges 10:6–12:7

11. The judge Ibzan—Judges 12:8-10

12. The judge Elon—Judges 12:11-12

13. The judge Abdon—Judges 12:13-15

14. The judge Samson—Judges 13–16

15. The depravity of Israel: idolatry and immorality— Judges 17–18

16. Civil war among the tribes—Judges 19–21

The pattern of Israel's moral and spiritual defeat is set in the very first chapter of Judges. There we read that "the people of Benjamin did not drive out the Jebusites who lived in Jerusalem" (1:21), the tribe of "Manasseh did not drive out the inhabitants of Beth-shean and its villages" (1:27), the tribe of "Ephraim did not drive out the

Canaanites who lived in Gezer" (1:29), the tribe of "Zebulun did not drive out the inhabitants of Kitron" (1:30), "the Asherites lived among the Canaanites, the inhabitants of the land, for they did not drive them out" (1:32), the tribe of "Naphtali did not drive out the inhabitants" (1:33), and on and on.

Why did the tribes of Israel fail to carry out God's command? Apparently, many Israelites found it more profitable to exploit the Canaanites than to drive them out, as we see in 1:28: "When Israel grew strong, they put the Canaanites to forced labor, but did not drive them out completely." The Israelites didn't take God seriously when he warned against the moral and spiritual pollution of the Canaanites and their idols. So the Israelites mingled with the Canaanites, traded with them, sometimes enslaved them, and eventually began to intermarry with them and worship pagan idols with them—fulfilling God's warning.

The Israelites set themselves up for decline and collapse when they failed to obey God's commandments. They settled for half a victory.

Before we judge the Israelites too harshly, we need to examine ourselves and ask: Have we settled for half a victory over our sin and self-defeating habits? Have we driven out our bad habits of gossip, lust, bitterness, anger, foul language, or addiction? Do we excuse our vices or are we committed to complete victory over them by driving them out of our lives? These "small" compromises (at least we like to think of them as small) are an accommodation with the enemy. We are symbolically mingling and intermarrying with the Canaanites—and if we do not drive them out, we will end up defeated.

Israel's Defection

We see how these supposedly small compromises led the people of Israel into the depths of degradation and defection in Judges 2:

Now the angel of the LORD went up from Gilgal to Bochim. And he said, "I brought you up from Egypt and brought you into the land that I swore to give to your fathers. I said, 'I will never break my covenant with you, and you shall make no covenant with the inhabitants of this land; you shall break down their altars.' But you have not obeyed my voice. What is this you have done? So now I say, I will not drive them out before you, but they shall become thorns in your sides, and their gods shall be a snare to you" (2:1-3).

Even though the people of Israel received a warning directly from an angel of the Lord, they chose to defect from faith in God and to degrade themselves with false gods:

And the people of Israel did what was evil in the sight of the LORD and served the Baals. And they abandoned the LORD, the God of their fathers, who had brought them out of the land of Egypt. They went after other gods, from among the gods of the peoples who were around them, and bowed down to them. And they provoked the LORD to anger. They abandoned the LORD and served the Baals and the Ashtaroth (2:11-13).

Baal was the male fertility god of the Canaanites, and Ashtaroth was the Canaanite fertility goddess. The Israelites were well aware of the Ten Commandments, which begin:

"You shall have no other gods before me.

"You shall not make for yourself a carved image, or any likeness of anything that is in heaven above, or that is in the earth beneath, or that is in the water under the earth. You shall not bow down to them or serve them, for I the LORD your God am a jealous God" (Exodus 20:3-5a).

When the Israelites started down the road of spiritual defection, they never imagined they would end up violating the First Commandment. They only intended to make a few compromises with sin. They knew God had told them to drive out the Canaanites, but they were confident that enslaving the Canaanites and exploiting their forced labor would be even better than driving them out.

In time, just as God had warned them, they were soon partaking in the idolatry of the Canaanites—an idolatry that was connected with the obscene fertility rites and sexual practices of the Canaanites. The Israelites didn't merely bow down before idols of stone and brass. They also engaged in the horrible and indescribable immorality of the Canaanites. They descended to such a state of moral and spiritual bankruptcy that God had no choice but to discipline the nation of Israel for its disobedience:

> So the anger of the LORD was kindled against Israel, and he gave them over to plunderers, who plundered them. And he sold them into the hand of their surrounding enemies, so that they could no longer withstand their enemies. Whenever they marched out, the hand of the LORD was against them for harm, as the LORD had warned, and as the LORD had sworn to them. And they were in terrible distress (2:14-15).

The hand of the Lord was against the people of Israel. Why, because God hated the Israelites? No! It was because God loved them. God didn't want to destroy his people but to save them from their foolishness and sin. So he showed the Israelites that as long as they disobeyed him and worshiped false gods, nothing in their lives would work out right. They would march off to war and face defeat. The tribes they had once enslaved now enslaved them and ruled over them.

The Twelve Judges

The Israelites found themselves in terrible distress—and out of their distress, they cried out to God. Then God in his grace sent Israel a series of deliverers called *judges*:

> Then the LORD raised up judges, who saved them out of the hand of those who plundered them. Yet they did not listen to their judges, for they whored after other gods and bowed down to them. They soon turned aside from the way in which their fathers had walked, who had obeyed the commandments of the LORD, and they did not do so. Whenever the LORD raised up judges for them, the LORD was with the judge, and he saved them from the hand of their enemies all the days of the judge. For the LORD was moved to pity by their groaning because of those who afflicted and oppressed them (2:16-18).

Even after the people of Israel sinned grievously against God, he graciously sent them judges to deliver them. Did the people of Israel learn from their past sins and defections? The book of Judges records the tragic and ungrateful response of the people to God's gracious deliverance:

> But whenever the judge died, they turned back and were more corrupt than their fathers, going after other gods, serving them and bowing down to them. They did not drop any of their practices or their stubborn ways (2:19).

Not only did the people of Israel repeat the pattern of disobedience, but with each cycle, they descended into worse and worse sin and corruption. Whenever a judge died, the people became even *more* corrupt than their fathers had been. In all, God raised up twelve judges over Israel—eleven men and one woman:

The judge *Othniel* (3:9-11). The people of Israel were oppressed and enslaved for eight years by Cushan-rishathaim, king of Mesopotamia. Then God raised up Othniel, a nephew of the great Israelite hero Caleb. Othniel led Israel into battle, ended the oppression of the Mesopotamians, and ushered in forty years of peace. That era of peace ended when Israel was defeated by Eglon, king of Moab.

The judge *Ehud* (3:11-29). After the Israelites had suffered eighteen years of oppression under the Moabites, God raised up Ehud. This judge and deliverer went to King Eglon to bring him the annual payment that Moab demanded from Israel. Being a left-handed man, Ehud was able to hide a double-edged short sword on his right thigh, where the Moabites would not think to look. When Ehud was alone with King Eglon, he said, "I have a message from God for you." Then he drew the sword and plunged it into the body of the king of Moab, and the king was so grossly overweight that the short sword went into him, hilt and all. By the time the king's attendants found Eglon dead, Ehud was miles away. He rallied the Israelite tribes and led them to victory against the leaderless Moabites—and there was peace in Israel for eighty years.

The judge *Shamgar* (3:31). The description of Shamgar, the son of Anath, is tantalizingly brief. One other brief mention of Shamgar in Judges 5:6 tells us that crime was rampant when God raised him up as a judge. The Scriptures tell us that "the highways were abandoned, and travelers kept to the byways." There is no introduction or conclusion to the story of Shamgar, nor is there any indication how long he was a judge in Israel. We are told only that Shamgar "killed 600 of the Philistines with an oxgoad, and he also saved Israel."

The judge *Deborah* (chapters 4–5). The only woman judge mentioned in Scripture, Deborah rallied the Israelites and led a victorious attack against the Canaanite king Jabin and his army commander, Sisera. Deborah brought forty years of peace to Israel. We will examine her story in detail in this book.

The judge *Gideon* (chapters 6–8). After the four decades of peace following the victory of Deborah, Israel was oppressed by the Midianites and Amalekites. So God raised up Gideon from the tribe of Manasseh and commanded him to remove idol worship from Israel and to free the people from foreign oppression. Gideon was initially insecure and reluctant to trust God's command, so he asked God for three forms of miraculous proof that this command truly came from God—and God supplied the proof. In obedience to God, Gideon reduced his army from thirty-two thousand men to a mere three hundred, and though vastly outnumbered, Israel defeated the Midianites by God's power. Gideon is named in Hebrews 11 as a great role model of faith. We will examine his story in detail.

The judges *Tola* (10:1-2) and *Jair* (10:3-5). The book of Judges tells us little of these two men. We know that Tola was a judge in Israel for twenty-three years and Jair the Gileadite judged Israel for twenty-two years.

The judge *Jephthah* (11:1–12:7). Jephthah delivered Israel by leading the army of Israel to victory over the Ammonites. The son of a prostitute, Jephthah was driven from home by his half-brothers, the legitimate sons of his father, Gilead. But when the Ammonites attacked, the elders of Gilead sent for Jephthah and put him in charge of the army. As Jephthah prepared to go to war against the Ammonites, he vowed to God, "If you will give the Ammonites into my hand, then whatever comes out from the doors of my house to meet me when I return in peace from the Ammonites shall be the LORD's, and I will offer it up for a burnt offering" (Judges 11:30b-31).

Jephthah was victorious—but when he returned home, the first living creature he saw was his daughter, his only child, dancing in his honor. Bound by his vow, Jephthah tore his clothes and wept, and he gave his daughter two months' grace before carrying out his vow. Jephthah's daughter graciously accepted her fate, saying, "My father, you have opened your mouth to the LORD; do to me according to what has gone out of your mouth, now that the LORD has avenged you on your enemies, on the Ammonites" (11:37). She and her friends went into the mountains to mourn that she would never marry. After two months, she returned to her father "who did with her according to his vow that he had made" (11:39).

The standard interpretation of this last statement is that Jephthah sacrificed his daughter, though it is not entirely certain that he did so. The text doesn't specifically tell us that he killed her. The statement that whatever he meets "shall be the LORD's, *and* I will offer it up for a burnt offering" could also be translated "shall be the LORD's, *or* I will offer it up for a burnt offering." In other words, Jephthah might have dedicated his daughter to a life of chastity and lifelong virginity. Jephthah would surely have known that human sacrifice, which was associated with the false religion of the pagans, is detestable to the Lord under the law of Moses (see Deuteronomy 12:31; 18:9-12). So while Jepthah's vow was certainly foolish and tragic for his daughter, it might have resulted in her remaining chaste for life instead of resulting in her death.

The judges *Ibzan* (12:8-10), *Elon* (12:11), and *Abdon* (12:13-15). Little is written about these three judges. Ibzan was a judge in Israel for seven years and was buried in Bethlehem (though there is some question whether he was buried in Bethlehem of Judah, where Jesus

was born, or Bethlehem of Zebulun in Galilee). Elon was a judge in
Israel for ten years, and Abdon was a judge for eight years. The historian Josephus mentions Abdon and tells us that Israel was at peace
during his tenure as judge.

The judge *Samson* (chapters 13–16). The story of Samson is dealt
with at length in Judges, and we will take a close look at his life. Samson's birth was prophesied by an angel, who told his parents that he
would begin to deliver the Israelites from the Philistine oppressors.
At the time that Samson was born, Israel had suffered under the Philistines for forty years. Samson's parents dedicated him to God and
to keeping the Nazirite vows. These vows are described in Numbers
6:1-21 (the Hebrew word *nāzîr* from which we get *Nazirite* means
"consecrated").

God blessed Samson and the Spirit of God was on him. More-
over, the Holy Spirit gave Samson amazing strength—the strength
to kill a young lion that attacked him and tear it to pieces, the
strength to kill thirty Philistine men in Ashkelon, and the strength
to kill a thousand Philistine soldiers while he was armed only with
the jawbone of a donkey.

But Samson foolishly told the spy Delilah the secret of his
strength. She betrayed Samson to the Philistine oppressors, and the
Philistines put out his eyes and made him a slave in Gaza. In the end,
the Philistines gathered in the temple of Dagon to make sacrifices
to their pagan deity in gratitude for delivering their hated enemy,
Samson, into their hands. Leaning against the central pillars of the
temple, Samson prayed to God for strength—then he dislodged the
pillars with his bare hands, killing the Philistine rulers and about
three thousand other Philistines. After his death, his family took his
body and buried him in the tomb of Manoah his father.

Your Deliverer

In the time of the judges, God always sent Israel a deliverer to rescue them from the consequences of their sin and folly. The people of Israel went through cycle after cycle of defection, discipline, and deliverance. They didn't have to continually wobble from deliverance to defection and back again, but that was how they chose to live. The Israelites had free will and could have chosen obedience to God. Instead, they chose to compromise with sin.

That's the tragic lesson of the book of Judges. If we don't want to follow the same pattern, we need to take God's commands seriously. No longer can we accommodate ourselves to sin and to the surrounding culture. God calls us to drive those self-defeating habits out of our lives. We need to live lives that are distinct from the world around us, lives that are distinctly Christian and Christlike. If we fail to take God's Word seriously, if we choose to flirt with sin instead of dealing with it, firmly and decisively, we will end up like the Israelites, repeatedly bringing sorrow and suffering upon ourselves.

As we read through Judges, we see that the judges were not superspiritual saints. Some of them were deeply flawed. Several serve more as warnings than as role models. Samson's pursuit of pagan women shows an amazing lapse of judgment on his part. God had repeatedly warned the Israelites against being "unequally yoked" (as Paul puts it in 2 Corinthians 6:14) with unbelievers, and Samson's parents pleaded with him to stay away from Philistine women. But Samson was not only strong, he was headstrong, and he did what was right in his own eyes. He ultimately paid a heavy price for his willfulness.

The story of Jephthah also serves as a warning to others. Never make a rash vow, because you may have to keep it, to your own sorrow and regret. Whether Jephthah sacrificed his daughter's physical life or her future happiness by committing her to a celibate lifestyle, his reckless vow was costly for both of them. Don't make promises you cannot keep, and don't swear an oath. In all your dealings with God and with other people, let your yes be yes and your no be no.

The key insight of Judges appears twice in the book: "In those days there was no king in Israel. Everyone did what was right in his own eyes" (17:6 and 21:25). It is rightly said that the road to hell is paved with good intentions. The people of Israel did not set out to do evil. They wanted to do right—but they did what was right in their own eyes. They did what was right according to human wisdom, but they neglected the wisdom of God.

That is the theme of Judges. It's a warning we will bear in mind as we take a closer look at three important figures from this book—Deborah, Gideon, and Samson.

2

Beware of
Spiritual Amnesia

Richard Dawkins is an evolutionary biologist and a leading atheist. In his 2006 book *The God Delusion*, Professor
Dawkins contends that belief in God is a delusion, a false
and harmful belief—and he asserts that teaching faith in God to
our children amounts to psychological child abuse. He quotes a
colleague, evolutionary psychologist Nicholas Humphrey, who, in
a 1997 Oxford lecture, said:

> Freedom of speech is too precious a freedom to be med-
> dled with...I shall probably shock you when I say it is
> the purpose of my lecture today to argue in one particu-
> lar area just the opposite...I am talking about moral and
> religious education. And especially the education a child
> receives at home...

Children, I'll argue, have a human right not to have their minds crippled by exposure to other people's bad ideas— no matter who these other people are. Parents, correspondingly, have no god-given licence to enculturate their children in whatever ways they personally choose: no right to limit the horizons of their children's knowledge, to bring them up in an atmosphere of dogma and superstition, or to insist they follow the straight and narrow paths of their own faith.

In short, children have a right not to have their minds addled by nonsense. And we as a society have a duty to protect them from it. So we should no more allow parents to teach their children to believe, for example, in the literal truth of the Bible...than we should allow parents to knock their children's teeth out or lock them in a dungeon.[1]

These are shocking words indeed. Here are two respected scientists who consider religious instruction to be a form of child abuse and who openly advocate that Christian parents be forbidden, presumably by the state, from transmitting their faith to the next generation. Why? Because these members of the scientific elite have determined that the Christian faith "cripples" a child's mind with "dogma and superstition."

Have these atheists forgotten that we have already conducted this experiment? We have created human societies in which parents are forbidden to transmit their Christian faith and Christian values to the next generation. I refer, of course, to Communist societies.

Journalist Peter Hitchens (the devoutly Christian brother of the late atheist spokesman Christopher Hitchens) spent five years as a correspondent in the old Soviet Union, shortly before the collapse of

Communism. In his 2010 book *The Rage Against God*, Peter Hitchens described life in "Communist, atheist, humanist Moscow" as "harsh and dangerous…coarse and mannerless," in contrast to the "good manners of a rich and stable Protestant Christian society." He noted that while Western nations in the Christian tradition are ruled by freedom, atheist Communist nations are ruled by fear. All the necessary commodities of life are in short supply, and supplies are manipulated by the Communist central planners to maintain fear and control. Neighbors spy on neighbors and pass information to the secret police in exchange for official favors.

Peter Hitchens describes the harsh conditions into which children were born and raised in the old Soviet Union:

> Even for the married, the main form of family planning…was abortion…In 1990, there were 6.46 million abortions in the USSR and 4.85 million live births. Birth itself was an authoritarian ordeal, with the newborns snatched away from their mothers by scowling nurses…and denied breast or bottle until the set time came around…
>
> Once the baby was home, married life quickly included the state as third parent, since salaries were carefully set so that it took two wages to pay for the basics of life. It was virtually unknown for any mother to stay at home to look after her children, who were placed very early in slovenly nurseries…[Soviet children were] rarely given anything resembling a Western mother's loving attention.[2]

Child rearing in the Soviet totalitarian state was conducted exactly as Richard Dawkins and Nicholas Humphrey say it should be. Soviet schools were indoctrination centers for atheist, secularist propaganda, and parents were not permitted to bring up their children in their own beliefs. As one Soviet education theorist stated in 1918:

> Children, like soft wax, are very malleable and they should be moulded into good Communists...We must rescue children from the harmful influence of the family...From the earliest days of their little lives, they must find themselves under the beneficent influence of Communist schools...To oblige the mother to give her child to the Soviet state—that is our task.[3]

The old Soviet Union may be dead, but social commentator Dennis Prager warns that "the secular indoctrination of a generation" goes on—and it is happening in America and throughout Western civilization. Prager writes:

> The average young person in the Western world is immersed in a secular cocoon. From elementary school through graduate school, only one way of looking at the world—the secular—is presented. The typical individual in the Western world receives as secular an indoctrination as the typical European received a religious one in the Middle Ages. I have taught college students and have found that their ignorance not only of the Bible but of the most elementary religious arguments and concepts—such as the truism that if there is no God, morality is subjective—is total.[4]

We are engaged in a struggle for the hearts and souls of our children. We face an elite intelligentsia and an increasingly powerful state, both of which seek to strip us of the God-ordained right and duty to raise our children in "the nurture and admonition of the

Lord" (Ephesians 6:4 KJV). This is a right we must never surrender, a duty we must never neglect. The life and eternal destiny of your child depends on your commitment to raising that child in the Christian faith.

God calls us to teach the next generation, transmit our faith to the next generation, equip the next generation, and above all, pray for the next generation. This is the only cure for what I call "mass spiritual amnesia"—a culture-wide memory loss. One of Satan's key tactics in his spiritual war against us is the attempt to erase the memory of God's truth from the minds of our children.

The peril of spiritual amnesia is a central theme of the book of Judges.

The Satanic Strategy

Of all the books I have written, this book may be the most urgent, practical, and important. The book of Judges deals with the spiritual crisis we face today in our families and churches—a crisis of spiritual amnesia. As I look at our world, our secular and post-Christian culture, and our increasingly rudderless church, I see a mirror image of events that took place during the period of the judges.

Just as generations of Israelites in that era repeatedly fell away from God's commandments, our generation is falling away from its biblical foundation. As a culture, we have ceased to look for answers from the Word of God. Our schools and universities—many of which were founded as institutions of Christian instruction—no longer take the Bible seriously.

Atheists revise history, falsely portraying great Bible-believing heroes of American history—Washington, Adams, Lincoln, and others—as atheists and secular humanists. For example, atheists quote the second president of the United States, John Adams, as saying, "This would be the best of all possible worlds, if there were no religion in it!!!" And he did, in fact, write those words in a letter to Thomas Jefferson—exclamation points and all. But he wrote them to *refute* them. In context, Adams wrote:

> Twenty times, in the course of my late Reading, have I been upon the point of breaking out, "This would be the best of all possible Worlds, if there were no Religion in it!!!" But in this exclamation I should have been as fanatical as Bryant or Cleverly [a reference to Adams's boyhood minister Lemuel Bryant and Latin schoolmaster Joseph Cleverly]. Without Religion this World would be Something not fit to be mentioned in polite Company, I mean Hell.[5]

Adams is saying he's sometimes tempted, because of the hypocrisy he's seen in religious people, to think the world would be better off without religion. But the atheists who quote Adams omit his true belief, stated in the concluding sentence, that a world without the Christian faith would be truly hellish. So don't be taken in by dishonest "quotations" served up by atheists and secularists. America was founded on sound Christian principles by Bible-believing people.

The satanic forces of this world are trying to cut us off from our heritage of faith and rob us of the truth—*and the satanic strategy is working.* Churches that once proclaimed the essence of the gospel of Jesus Christ—namely, that Jesus alone saves—are now a dwindling minority. A 2008 survey released by the Pew Forum on Religion and Public Life revealed that 70 percent of all Americans believe there are many religious paths to God and eternal life. This includes 65 percent of all self-identified Christians and 56 percent of all evangelicals.[6] How can a person claim to be an evangelical Christian while denying the Lord's own claim (in John 14:6) to be the only way to God the Father? If Jesus is not the only way to God, then why did he have to die on the cross?

That's why the book of Judges is so instructive for us today. It's a warning to us whether we are single or married, whether we are parents or grandparents or have no children of our own. If we fail to transmit our faith and values to the next generation, our culture and our nation will suffer the same fate as ancient Israel.

Don't Become Canaanized

At the beginning of Judges 2, God sends an angel to shake the people of Israel out of their spiritual amnesia:

> Now the angel of the LORD went up from Gilgal to Bochim. And he said, "I brought you up from Egypt and brought you into the land that I swore to give to your fathers. I said, 'I will never break my covenant with you, and you shall make no covenant with the inhabitants of this land; you shall break down their altars.' But you have not obeyed my voice. What is this you have done? So now I say, I will not drive them out before you, but they shall become thorns in your sides, and their gods shall be a snare to you." As soon as the angel of the LORD spoke these words to all the people of Israel, the people lifted up their voices and wept. And they called the name of that place Bochim. And they sacrificed there to the LORD (2:1-5).

The angel gives God's message to the people of Israel, reminding them of the covenant God has made with them—and of their disobedience. The angel's words hit the mark. The people are shaken from their spiritual amnesia, they remember the covenant between God and Israel, and they weep in repentance for having broken the covenant. As a reminder of their repentance, they name the place Bochim, which means "weepers."

This passage shows us the lengths God will go to in extending mercy to his people. He actually sent an angel to remind them of all he had done for them and of the covenant he had made with them. The people of Israel were spiritual amnesiacs, and they had forgotten God's love for them.

The people of that generation did not set out to defy God or openly rebel against him. They continued to be religiously observant. They continued to do charitable works. They went through the motions of their religion.

But they had squeezed the truth of who God is to the margins of their lives. They didn't deny Yahweh or remove him from their society. They simply pushed him off to the side and denied him his central place. They wanted to worship God, but they also wanted to enjoy the Canaanite ways.

God had commanded Israel to eliminate the Canaanites (see Deuteronomy 20:16-18). But the Israelites could not bring themselves to do as God commanded. Instead, they found much to admire about the Canaanites. They cozied up to the Canaanites, exchanged agricultural and metalworking ideas, and even incorporated some of the Canaanite religious practices into their worship of Yahweh. In short, God's chosen people became Canaanized.

The seeds of Israel's decline began with spiritual compromise— the same kind of spiritual compromise we now see throughout America. Our churches are compromising the truth of the gospel. Even many self-proclaimed evangelical Christians are compromising biblical truth and morality.

Many Christians today are like the Israelites who looked at the people around them and said, "What's so bad about these Canaanites? They seem like nice people. I wonder why God would tell us we should eliminate them and never intermarry with them. Their men are strong and handsome. Their women are beautiful. Sure, they worship idols instead of Yahweh, but we should be tolerant and open-minded. I know God said we should have no other gods before him, but who are we to think we have the corner on truth? I'm sure there are many paths that lead to the same destination. Besides, I wouldn't want anyone to think I'm intolerant."

In truth, our God is an intolerant God—and rightfully so. He tells us, "You shall not make for yourself a carved image, or any likeness of anything that is in heaven above, or that is in the earth beneath, or that is in the water under the earth. You shall not bow down to them or serve them, for I the LORD your God am a jealous God" (Exodus 20:4-5a). That is an intolerant statement by a righteously intolerant God. That's what he means when he tells us he is a "jealous" God. He will not share his people with other gods. He will not tolerate idolatry.

Tolerance is not always a virtue. Showing tolerance toward sin, idolatry, blasphemy, demonic practices, and immorality is no virtue at all. Such tolerance is an offense to God, and it should be an offense to you and to me.

When Christians tolerate evil, when they allow moral lines to become blurred, then Christ is dethroned as Lord. Once he is relegated to being just one way to God among many, once he is no longer *the* way, *the* truth, *the* life, and the *only* way to God the Father, moral relativism is sure to follow. Once Christianity becomes just another religious philosophy—like the eightfold path of Buddhism, the five pillars of Islam, the dharma of Hinduism, or the bridge to total freedom of Scientology—the seeds of destruction have been planted. The authentic Christian faith is not a moral principle or a spiritual practice. It's a relationship with the One who is the only way to eternal life.

If the book of Judges teaches us anything, it teaches that we must never give an inch to false religions, we must never settle for partial victories over sin, we must never give up our spiritual birthright, and we must never forget our spiritual heritage. Departure from the truth is never inevitable. We must always contend for every soul and pray intensely for our children and our children's children. We must stand firm for future generations so they will never fall prey to spiritual amnesia.

The Art of Spiritual Warfare[7]

The Bible tells us that children are a heritage from the Lord (see Psalm 127:3). Our children do not belong to us. God has placed them in our care. We are stewards of these precious souls God has entrusted to us. And one of the key responsibilities we have as stewards of these children is to train them for the battle, for spiritual warfare.

It's important that we understand that our enemy, the devil, is not very creative. Satan is not an original thinker and he has no new ideas. If you study the Bible and human history, you'll see that he has only one trick up his sleeve, and he relies on it over and over again. In every generation, he dresses it up and tries to sell it as a new idea, but it's the same deception he used in the Garden of Eden. In Genesis 3:1, Satan said to Eve, "Did God actually say, 'You shall not eat of any tree in the garden'?"

In other words, "Did you really understand what God was saying? Are you sure God's Word really means what you think it means? What if you misinterpreted his command?"

Satan used this same trick on the generation of Joshua. After God had led Israel out of bondage in Egypt, through the Red Sea and the Jordan River, through one victory after another, Satan spoke to the Israelite people. His message was: "Are you sure you heard God correctly? Are you sure God really wants you to be so intolerant of other people and other faiths? You know, these Canaanite gods have a lot to offer. They are gods and goddesses of nature, of fertility, of pleasure. Surely God would want you to receive the blessings that come from worshiping these other gods."

And Satan is using this same trick on our generation today. He's whispering into the ears of church members, pastors, seminarians, and Bible teachers, "Are you sure you are interpreting the Bible correctly? Are you sure the stories of creation, Adam and Eve, Noah, Moses, and Joshua are still believable in this scientific age? You know, the evolutionary scientists seem awfully sure of Darwinism. Maybe we should simply embrace evolution as a fact and treat the Bible as an allegory—filled with helpful insights, but not to be taken seriously as history."

Please hear me on this: Just as the devil succeeded in deceiving the generation of the Judges by convincing the Israelites that they could have Yahweh and the fertility gods of the Canaanites as well, the devil is deceiving our generation, saying that Christians can have Jesus and evolution as well.

In February 2012, atheist Richard Dawkins and the then-archbishop of Canterbury, Rowan Williams, met at Oxford University for a debate on human origins. Both Dawkins and Williams affirmed that they believed in Darwinian evolution. Since Archbishop Williams believes in Darwinian evolution, he had to affirm that the first human beings—Adam and Eve, according to the Scriptures—must have had nonhuman ancestors, even though the Bible states that they had no ancestors whatsoever. When asked to explain how he could square a belief in Darwinian evolution with a belief in God, the archbishop said,

> From where I start, there has to be a point in the [Creation] story at which the proto-human becomes conscious of what I'll call a calling from God or an address from God. I'm wary of saying that God somehow bends down and tinkers with the machinery. But there is a point, if you like, implicit in the whole process from the beginning, a point at which it will be possible for that proto-human to be conscious in another way, including the consciousness of the Divine. And that, I would say, is the beginning of what I would regard as humanity in the image of God.[8]

You can read that statement again and again, and I doubt you will learn how to reconcile the theory of evolution with the truth of God's Word. In fact, if you can make sense of it at all, please explain it to me! Professor Dawkins, the atheist, will tell you plainly that evolution and the Bible are irreconcilable. I find it ironic that on this point, I actually agree more with the atheist than with the former leader of the Church of England.

William B. Provine is a science historian and professor at Cornell University. He is also a devout atheist who once said, "Evolution is the greatest engine of atheism ever invented."[9] In a debate with Phillip E. Johnson at Stanford University, Dr. Provine candidly explained the implications of Darwinian evolution:

> Let me summarize my views on what modern evolutionary biology tells us loud and clear—and these are basically Darwin's views. There are no gods, no purposes,

and no goal-directed forces of any kind. There is no life after death. When I die, I am absolutely certain that I am going to be dead. That's the end of me. There is no ultimate foundation for ethics, no ultimate meaning in life, and no free will for humans, either.[10]

Once you accept evolution as a fact, it will not take very long before Jesus, the creator and sustainer of the universe, will be lost in the shuffle. Why do you think the secular forces are becoming more and more militant in defending evolution and attacking Christianity, religious freedom, and the teachings of the Bible?

Satan is fighting, cruelly and relentlessly, for the souls of our children. And that's why we must teach our children the art of spiritual warfare. As parents, we are their role models, and we must allow them to watch us and learn from us as we do spiritual battle. It's not enough to give our children a good education, a good financial start in life, and a pat on the back. To do so is to send our children into spiritual war without armor, without weapons, and without training for battle.

The apostle Paul tells us as parents to train our children and "bring them up in the discipline and instruction of the Lord" (Ephesians 6:4b). Then, a few verses later, Paul writes about the nature of the battle that we and our children face. He urges us to "be strong in the Lord and in the strength of his might. Put on the whole armor of God, that you may be able to stand against the schemes of the devil. For we do not wrestle against flesh and blood, but against the rulers, against the authorities, against the cosmic powers over this present darkness, against the spiritual forces of evil in the heavenly places" (Ephesians 6:10b-12).

Then he describes "the whole armor of God" that enables us to stand firm in the battle: the belt of truth, the breastplate of righteousness, the shoes of the gospel of peace, the shield of faith (to extinguish Satan's flaming darts), the helmet of salvation, the sword of the Spirit (which is the Word of God), and the power of prayer (see Ephesians 6:13-18). This is how we equip our children and prepare them for battle. We equip them with the authority of the Word of God. We are committed to seeing our children win the only battle that truly matters—the battle for their eternal souls.

Model the mindset and behavior of a spiritual warrior. Drench their minds with the truth of God's Word. Spend time with them, talk to them, listen to them, and dialogue with them about spiritual matters. Cry to God on their behalf. Raise your children in such a way that they will be able to say, along with King David, "He trains my hands for war, so that my arms can bend a bow of bronze" (2 Samuel 22:35).

Blood on Our Hands

The book of Judges serves as a warning, but it also serves as an encouragement for our faith. It demonstrates to us the relentless grace of God. Over and over, he delivers the people of Israel from their folly and sin. That is a great encouragement to our hearts today. In the stories of the book of Judges, we see that our God of grace does not give up. He never lets us down and never lets us go. He pursues us and continually draws us back to him.

The book of Judges picks up precisely where the book of Joshua leaves off. Near the end of his life, Joshua said, "Choose this day whom you will serve, whether the gods your fathers served in the region beyond the River, or the gods of the Amorites in whose land you dwell. But as for me and my house, we will serve the LORD" (Joshua 24:15b). When the people of Israel confidently responded, "We also will serve the LORD," Joshua intensified his warning, saying,

"You are not able to serve the LORD, for he is a holy God" (Joshua 24:19b).

Joshua seemed to foresee the repeated cycle of failure that would be recorded in the book of Judges. Yet he also bequeathed to Israel a legacy of faith and faithfulness. He gave Israel a vision of a bright future if the people would put away their foreign gods and incline their hearts to the God of Israel. If Israel would be faithful to God, then God would continue to fight their battles and give them land they had not labored for, cities they had not built, and vineyards and olive orchards they did not plant.

But each subsequent generation must learn from the previous generation. After Joshua dies, the people of Israel commit a grievous error:

> When Joshua dismissed the people, the people of Israel went each to his inheritance to take possession of the land. And the people served the LORD all the days of Joshua, and all the days of the elders who outlived Joshua, who had seen all the great work that the LORD had done for Israel. And Joshua the son of Nun, the servant of the LORD, died at the age of 110 years. And they buried him within the boundaries of his inheritance in Timnath-heres, in the hill country of Ephraim, north of the mountain of Gaash. And all that generation also were gathered to their fathers. And there arose another generation after them who did not know the LORD or the work that he had done for Israel (Judges 2:6-10).

A generation arose that was utterly ignorant of all that God had done for Israel. Why was this generation ignorant? Because their parents failed to pass down their heritage of faith. Their parents neglected to bring up their children in the nurture and admonition of the Lord. Faith in God cannot be transmitted genetically. It cannot be absorbed by osmosis. Faith must be intentionally taught and transmitted from one generation to the next.

In America, many Christians of the "Greatest Generation"—the generation that endured the Great Depression and fought World War II—failed to teach the next generation, the Baby Boomer generation. They failed to pass on to the Boomers the all-important art of spiritual warfare. As a result, the Baby Boomer generation had nothing to pass along to the next generation. That is why younger generations today are spiritually stunted, biblically illiterate, and woefully unprepared for spiritual battle.

I don't say this to assign blame or find fault. The only reason for looking back is to learn the lessons of the past and apply those lessons to the future. My goal is to prescribe the remedy for spiritual amnesia—because once spiritual amnesia sets in, compromise and spiritual decline surely follow.

Before I blame anyone else, I look in a mirror. I have to confess that my generation of Christians let down the next generation. We who stand in our churches' pulpits have failed the next generation. We have ceased to proclaim, "Thus says the Lord."

When Paul gave his farewell address to the Ephesian elders, he said, "Therefore I testify to you this day that I am innocent of the blood of all, for I did not shrink from declaring to you the whole counsel of God" (Acts 20:26-27). Can my generation of pastors say the same? Are we innocent of the blood of all? Or have we held back from declaring the whole counsel of God?

I fear that we who are called to shepherd God's flock have blood on our hands. We have failed to call people to repentance. We have focused on making people feel good so they will want to come back to church—and in so doing, we have failed to call sin "sin." We have failed to declare the whole counsel of God, and we have allowed an entire generation to grow up not knowing what sin and repentance are or what God expects of us. And we have sent that generation into the battle without armor, without weapons, without even informing them about the enemy they face.

If you are a mother or father, grandparent, teacher, coach, pastor, Sunday school teacher, or Christian mentor, you have a responsibility. You are called to pass a living testimony of God's grace to the next generation. You have influence with the next generation, and your influence confers on you a responsibility to train these young people for spiritual warfare. Don't send them into battle defenseless and unprepared.

You may think that moral relativism and secularism, postmodernism and political correctness are new concepts. In fact, these notions are as old as the book of Judges:

> And the people of Israel did what was evil in the sight of the LORD and served the Baals. And they abandoned the LORD, the God of their fathers, who had brought them out of the land of Egypt. They went after other gods, from among the gods of the peoples who were around them, and bowed down to them. And they provoked the LORD to anger. They abandoned the LORD and served the Baals and the Ashtaroth. So the anger of the LORD was kindled against Israel, and he gave them over to plunderers, who plundered them. And he sold them into the hand of their surrounding enemies, so that they could no longer withstand their enemies. Whenever they marched out, the hand of the LORD was against them for harm, as the LORD had warned, and as the LORD had sworn to them. And they were in terrible distress (2:11-15).

The Israelites were tolerant toward the Baals and the Ashtaroth (I'll talk more about this goddess a bit later in this chapter). They practiced moral and spiritual relativism. They were open-minded toward other religions and immoral lifestyles. Joshua's generation failed to train young people for battle, so the next generation lost the battle.

Drowning in Materialism and Debt

What is the job description of an Old Testament judge? If you're thinking of a judge sitting at the bench in black robes, such as a Supreme Court justice, that's not what an Old Testament judge was like. The Hebrew word translated "judge" in English actually meant "deliverer."

Old Testament judges delivered God's people from the messes they got themselves into. Throughout the book of Judges, we see the same scenario repeated again and again with exacting precision:

- *Step 1*: God's people become complacent in their peace and prosperity, and they compromise their faith.

- *Step 2*: The Lord's anger is kindled so he gives his people over to their oppressors.

- *Step 3*: The people cry to the Lord for help.

- *Step 4*: God raises a deliverer, a judge, to rescue them.

- *Step 5*: The cycle returns to *Step 1* and begins all over again.

But there is an important feature of this cycle that we dare not miss. If we read the book of Judges casually, we may overlook this all-important detail: With each revolution of the cycle, with each succeeding generation, there is a downward spiral. When this cycle returns to *Step 1*, we are not back where we started. The culture has slipped further into decline. Every succeeding time the people compromise their faith, they sink lower, they become more wicked and depraved, than the preceding generation.

We have seen this pattern played out in our own society. The history of Western civilization has been marked by periods of debauchery and decline, followed by revival and restoration.

For example, America enjoyed enormous post-World War I peace and prosperity in the era known as the "Roaring Twenties." Novelist F. Scott Fitzgerald wrote, "It was an age of excess"[11]—an excess of wealth, materialism, alcoholism, hedonism, and rebellion against God and traditional morality. It was a time of sexual "liberation" (that is, promiscuity) for women. Newspaper publisher William Randolph Hearst lived openly with his mistress, actress Marion Davies, and the immoral arrangement was accepted by the public and even by Hearst's wife. It was a time when homosexuality first became openly tolerated in the arts and entertainment communities. Hollywood actor William Haines was the top box office draw while living an openly homosexual lifestyle. Actress Mae West wrote and produced a 1926 play, *Sex*, celebrating prostitution, and a 1927 play, *The Drag*, celebrating homosexuality; both were hugely successful. During the 1920s, people rebelled against tradition—musical tradition (hence, "The Jazz Age"), gender roles (a popular 1926 song was "Masculine Women, Feminine Men"), and moral and religious tradition.

The arrogant, materialistic, self-confident spirit of the times was exemplified by the front-page headline of the *New York Times* on Sunday, October 13, 1929: "Stock Prices Will Stay at High Levels for Years to Come." Just eleven days later, on Thursday, October 24, the *Times* headlines read: "Prices of Stocks Crash" and "Many Accounts

Wiped Out."[12] The Roaring Twenties ended with the Crash of 1929, which ushered in the Great Depression. During the Depression and World War II, those who had thought the party would never end suddenly found their world was shaken and crumbling. The peace and prosperity of the Roaring Twenties came crashing down around them. Many people repented of their hedonism and depravity, turning to God for help and hope.

By any objective standard, America in the twenty-first century is a nation in spiritual and moral decline. Many observers date the beginning of American decline back to 1962, when the Supreme Court outlawed prayer in public schools. Others date it to 1973, when the Supreme Court legalized unrestricted abortion. These court decisions unleashed a tidal wave of harmful effects on our nation—not the least being the estimated fifty-six million human lives destroyed by legal abortion as of 2013.

But while court decisions can cause serious harm to society, it is truly the people themselves who determine the moral and spiritual strength of a nation. "We the People" can choose to say, "As for me and my house, we will serve the Lord." And "We the People" can also reject God and his truth. We choose whether or not to pray, to live righteously, to witness for Christ, and to raise our children in the nurture and admonition of the Lord.

Throughout the twentieth century, the vast majority of children were born into two-parent families. Having children outside of marriage was not only abnormal, it was considered shameful. And though it is not politically correct to say so, it *is* shameful. In 1964, 93 percent of American children were born to married couples. As of 2010, only 59 percent of American children are born in wedlock. The result of this moral decline: Children are forced into poverty. According to the US Census Bureau, the poverty rate for children in single-parent homes is 37.1 percent, compared with only 6.8 percent of children in two-parent homes. A child raised by two parents is *82 percent less likely to be in poverty* than a child raised by one parent.[13]

Another corrosive fact of American life is pornography. According to reliable estimates, 12 percent of sites on the Internet are pornographic, 25 percent of Internet searches are requests for pornography, 28,000 Internet users view porn at any given time, 43 percent of all Internet users visit pornographic sites from time to time, 266 new pornographic sites appear online each day, 3,000 English-language Internet sites distribute illegal child pornography, 70 percent of American children accidentally encounter Internet pornography while using the Internet for innocent purposes, and 34 percent of teenage girls and 15 percent of teenage boys have shared indecent photos or descriptions of themselves online.[14]

As the family breaks down in America, we are seeing a corresponding breakdown of America's moral fiber, especially the Protestant work ethic. The notion of the American dream was based on the idea that anyone could succeed in America if they were willing to work hard and play by the rules. Hard work creates wealth, a principle strongly affirmed in both the Old and New Testaments (see Proverbs 10:4; 12:11; 14:23; 16:3; 21:25; Ecclesiastes 9:10; Acts 20:35; Colossians 3:23; 2 Thessalonians 3:10). Working hard and creating wealth is a duty we have not only to ourselves and our families, but to the Lord and to our society. Today, fewer and fewer people are working and more and more people are living off the labor of the hard-working, tax-paying few. This is not just an economic or social problem; this is a moral and spiritual problem, and it is leading to the decline of our nation and our culture.

In 2001, America's gross domestic product accounted for 31.8

percent of all global economic activity. In 2011, a mere decade later, that figure had plummeted to 21.6 percent.[15] There are undoubtedly many reasons for this disturbing figure—but one of the reasons may well be that we are simply less productive and less hard-working as a people. There are too many people riding in the boat and not enough people rowing. In 1950, more than 80 percent of all American men were gainfully employed. Today, that number is less than 65 percent.[16] In 2008, 30.8 million Americans received food stamps; five years later, that number had swelled to 47.1 million.[17] A society cannot sustain itself while the percentage of its working, productive citizens steadily shrinks.

As individuals and as a society, we are drowning in debt. In 2001, the United States national debt totaled less than $6 trillion. The day this book is published, the national debt will exceed $18 trillion. Every single hour, we add an additional $100 million to the national debt. By 2016, the debt will top $20 trillion.[18]

Americans own more stuff than any society in the history of the planet—cars, boats, jet skis, TVs, video games, computers, smartphones, and other assorted luxury items. Yet the American people are swallowing antidepressants and other mood-altering drugs at an astounding rate, spending $60 billion more on prescription drugs in 2010 than they did just five years earlier.[19] We are entertaining and drugging ourselves into a stupor.

A Panreligious Perspective?

The tragedy of the church today is that we have identified with our dying culture instead of being distinct from it. In the Western church, we have fallen into Canaanite worship. Of course, we would never call it that, and we believe that we are worshiping Christ. But like the Israelites in the time of the judges, we have mingled false religion with our worship of the one true God.

Canaanite worship was earthy. It was largely concerned with the fertility of the earth and the prosperity that comes through worshiping Mother Earth and harvesting her fruitfulness. The Old Testament refers to this goddess as Ashtaroth—the goddess of fertility, sexuality, and war.

The land of Canaan in the time of the judges was an agrarian culture, and the economy of the region dependent on agriculture. Those who worshiped Ashtaroth believed their livelihood depended on keeping the goddess happy. An angry goddess was likely to send you drought, pestilence, and crop failure.

Today, Ashtaroth is called Mother Earth or Gaia. Whether in ancient times or in the twenty-first century, this deity is a demonic spirit masquerading as a goddess. In his book *Earth in the Balance*, former vice president Al Gore devotes a chapter, "Environmentalism of the Spirit," to promoting the worship of the earth as symbolized by Gaia. He writes:

> The richness and diversity of our religious tradition throughout history is a spiritual resource long ignored by people of faith, who are often afraid to open their minds to teachings first offered outside their own system of belief. But the emergence of a civilization in which knowledge moves freely and almost instantaneously through the world has...spurred a renewed investigation of the wisdom distilled by all faiths. This panreligious perspective may prove especially important where our global civilization's responsibility for the earth is concerned.[20]

Gore wants Christians to stop being so intolerant and to embrace a "panreligious perspective." That is, we should open ourselves to the teachings of *all* religions. And that's exactly what the Israelites did in the time of the judges.

Gore goes on to extol Native American religion and to quote the words of Chief Seattle to President Franklin Pierce in 1855, including the chief's question, "Will you teach your children what we have taught our children? That the earth is our mother?"[21] Al Gore also thinks it's unfortunate that the "last vestige of organized goddess worship was eliminated by Christianity as late as the fifteenth century in Lithuania."[22]

On October 9, 1993, Gore met with ministers from many denominations to create the National Religious Partnership for the Environment. One of those ministers was the Reverend James Parks Morton of the Cathedral of Saint John the Divine in New York. Reverend Morton once wrote, "The challenge before the religious community in America is to make every congregation—every church, synagogue and mosque—truly 'green'—a center of environmental study and action. That is their religious duty."[23]

That is not a statement of Christian faith. That is a statement of Canaanite religion. A church is a house of worship, and Reverend Morton says that our worship should be centered around "environmental study and action," and that this is our "religious duty." There is simply no biblical support for that view. You have to adopt Al Gore's "panreligious perspective" in order to come to such a conclusion.

The biblical perspective says that God created us to be good stewards of the earth. Genesis 1:31a tells us, "And God saw everything that he had made, and behold, it was very good," and Genesis 2:15 says, "The LORD God took the man and put him in the garden of

Eden to work it and keep it." In the original Hebrew, the phrase "to work it and keep it" connotes a responsibility to care for and protect the garden. But caring for the earth is a very different thing from worshiping the earth.

I want to be a good steward of God's creation. If you ask my family, they will tell you that I sometimes drive them crazy with my mania for recycling. I don't waste anything. I don't litter. When I go to the mountains or the shore, I try to leave the environment cleaner than when I found it. I pick up litter that was left by others. I think God is pleased when we are faithful stewards of his creation.

But God is not pleased when we worship his world, when we view the earth as a goddess. He is not pleased when we replace the worship of the one true God with Canaanite religion. He is not pleased when we water down the biblical faith he has given us with a "panreligious perspective." He is not pleased when, in our arrogance and hubris, we talk about how we must "save the earth." The notion that we can save the earth is a lie from the evil one, who said to the first woman, "You will be like God." We can't save the earth. Only the Savior can save the earth.

One of the great tragedies of our culture is that as we teach our children to love God the Father, our schools are indoctrinating our children to love Mother Earth. When we give creation the reverence that is due the Creator, we are guilty of Canaanite worship. Paul warns us that God's wrath is poured out on those who suppress the truth and who have "exchanged the truth about God for a lie and worshiped and served the creature rather than the Creator" (Romans 1:25b).

In the book of Judges, Israel descends into the folly of worshiping Canaanite idols alongside their worship of Yahweh. We commit the same error when we revere the creation alongside our reverence for the Creator. And we pass on this error to the next generation when we allow our children to be indoctrinated into a false religion that worships Mother Earth while rejecting God the Father.

The Avoidable Tragedy

John S. Dickerson, a pastor and the author of *The Great Evangelical Recession*, observes that evangelical Christianity is rapidly becoming a nonfactor in American elections. In 2012, he notes, "Americans voted in favor of same-sex marriage in four states, while Florida voters rejected an amendment to restrict abortion." During that year, he adds, "we witnessed a collapse in American evangelicalism." Polling by LifeWay Research and the Barna Group shows that "a majority of young people raised as evangelicals are quitting church, and often the faith, entirely." Dickerson concludes, "We evangelicals must accept that our beliefs are now in conflict with the mainstream culture. We cannot change ancient doctrines to adapt to the currents of the day."[24]

Dickerson's point is that we ought to be in conflict with our culture. If we are not at odds with our culture, then we are at odds with God. Remember the warning of James: "Do you not know that friendship with the world is enmity with God? Therefore whoever wishes to be a friend of the world makes himself an enemy of God" (James 4:4).

Some people look at the cultural decline all around us and call it progress. According to this progressive mindset, an enlightened and progressive society tolerates rampant abortion, pornography, sexual promiscuity, unwed parenting, same-sex marriage, indolence and dependence, and irresponsible, unsustainable debt. If we continue down the slope of moral and spiritual decline, we will suffer the same fate as Israel in the time of the judges. As Malcolm Muggeridge wrote so prophetically in *The End of Christendom*:

> I conclude that civilizations, like every other human creation, wax and wane. By the nature of the case there can never be a lasting civilization anymore than there can be a lasting spring or lasting happiness in an individual life or a lasting stability in a society. It's in the nature of man and of all that he constructs to perish, and it must ever be so. The world is full of the debris of past civilizations and others are known to have existed which have not left any debris behind them but have just disappeared.[25]

This noble experiment called America now appears headed for the ash heap of history, to lie alongside other failed kingdoms, empires, and republics of the past. America will not be conquered by invaders, destroyed by nuclear war, or dismembered by terrorists. If America passes away, it will be *destroyed from within* by the spiritual defection and moral compromise of her people, just as Israel was destroyed from within by compromise with the Canaanites.

The death of America will not mean the death of Christianity. Faith in Christ will go on. As G.K. Chesterton correctly observed, "Christianity has died many times and risen again; for it had a God who knew the way out of the grave." But the death of America as a moral and faithful nation will be an incomprehensible tragedy— a tragedy that we, like ancient Israel, could have avoided through faithfulness to God. That's why we must cry out to God for the next generation.

In Deuteronomy, God speaks affectionately of finding Israel in a desert land, in a howling wilderness, and God encircled the people of Israel and cared for them, keeping them as "the apple of his eye" (see Deuteronomy 32:10). But here in Judges, we sense the wounded heart of God as he grieves over his people for squeezing him out of the center of their lives. Here we see that God's most difficult battle is not with the pagans. It is with his own people.

God can deal with the pagans with a snap of his finger. But he agonizes over his rebellious children who turn their backs on him and use his grace as a license to sin. He grieves for his children who rationalize sin, who redefine marriage, who make excuses for the slaughter of innocent children, who call themselves Christians but follow lust, greed, and selfish ambition. He aches for those who name the name of Christ, but who live lives that are indistinguishable from the lives of the Canaanites.

Bequeathing a Heritage of Faith

Even though the story of the book of Judges is heartbreaking, its message is encouraging. The book records the history of Israel's failure. But it also records the message of God's grace. The book of Judges tells us that if we cry to God, if we repent and turn to him, he will extend grace to us—and not just to us but to the next generation:

> Then the LORD raised up judges, who saved them out of the hand of those who plundered them. Yet they did not listen to their judges, for they whored after other gods and bowed down to them. They soon turned aside from the way in which their fathers had walked, who had obeyed the commandments of the LORD, and they did not do so. Whenever the LORD raised up judges for them, the LORD was with the judge, and he saved them from the hand of their enemies all the days of the

judge. For the LORD was moved to pity by their groaning because of those who afflicted and oppressed them (2:16-18).

God raised up judges to deliver the people of Israel from their oppressors. God showed mercy and grace to the people of Israel, even after they had whored after the false Canaanite gods. But even after God showered them with mercy, the hearts of the people turned away from God and toward the Canaanite idols:

> But whenever the judge died, they turned back and were more corrupt than their fathers, going after other gods, serving them and bowing down to them. They did not drop any of their practices or their stubborn ways. So the anger of the LORD was kindled against Israel, and he said, "Because this people have transgressed my covenant that I commanded their fathers and have not obeyed my voice, I will no longer drive out before them any of the nations that Joshua left when he died, in order to test Israel by them, whether they will take care to walk in the way of the LORD as their fathers did, or not." So the LORD left those nations, not driving them out quickly, and he did not give them into the hand of Joshua (2:19-23).

If you think you are grieved by the decline of your culture, by the sin and immorality that surrounds you, by the suffering and sadness that pervades this fallen world, how much more must our loving Father grieve over us and our nation? Don't repeat the pattern of Israel in the days of the judges. Don't let your children, your grandchildren, or the children you teach and influence become another generation who did not know the Lord. Be faithful to God and

transmit your faith to the next generation. Here are some sugges-
tions for teaching your faith to the children you influence:

1. Worship with your children. This means more than merely going
to church together once a week. Begin a daily habit, in the morning or before bedtime (or both), of coming together for family worship. Read Bible stories together. Share your feelings of thankfulness,
prayer requests, and stories of what God is doing in your life. Sing
Christian songs together. Pray together. Discover the joy of daily
family worship.

2. Instruct your children. Find a family devotional book that is
appropriate for the age level of your children. Read Bible stories
together, then discuss them. Find ways to apply stories of the Bible
to the lives of your children. If a child is facing an intimidating challenge at school or in music lessons or in Little League, encourage
that child with a story about David and Goliath (1 Samuel 17), Daniel in the lion's den (Daniel 6), or Peter and John before the Sanhe-
drin (Acts 4).

3. Pray regularly with and for your children. Pray at meals and at
bedtime. Pray when your child is hurting. Thank God together during happy moments. Find ways to acknowledge God's presence so
that your children will continually be aware of his love and mercy
in their lives.

The Scottish Reformation leader John Knox was such a bold
man of faith that Mary, Queen of Scots, once said of him, "I fear
his prayers more than I do the armies of my enemies." In 1572, as
Knox lay on his deathbed, he called to his wife, Margaret, and said,
"Read me that Scripture where I first cast my anchor." She read to
him from John 17, the high priestly prayer of Jesus before he went
to the cross. That prayer comforted him, and he began to pray for
his family, for his fellow countrymen, for those who had rejected

the gospel, for those who had recently received the good news, for God's people who were facing persecution, for the wife and children he left behind, for future generations of believers.

Margaret listened as John prayed. His voice grew weaker and weaker until finally his lips ceased to move. John Knox died as he had lived, constantly interceding, continually praying, until he finally passed into the presence of his Lord. That is a great way to live, a great way to die, and a great way to bequeath a heritage of faith, godliness, and prayer to the next generation.

3

A Time for Decision

Pastor Mike Howerton grew up in Southern California. As a teenager, he and his friends would often go cliff jumping into Three Arch Bay at Laguna Beach. Being full of the bravado of youth, Howerton and his friends preferred jumping from the tallest of the three cliff faces. There were rocks at the base of the cliff, so a jumper would have to run and vault himself far enough from the cliff face to clear the rocks and hit the water. To make matters even more dangerous, there was very little running room atop the cliff, which was covered with slippery ice plant.

One day, one of Howerton's friends began his run to make his jump, but halfway to the cliff's edge, his nerve failed. He changed his mind and tried to stop—but his feet slipped on the ice plant and he went down, sliding toward the cliff's edge. His momentum drove him forward until his legs hung out over the edge of the cliff. For several awful seconds, he hung there, teetering over the edge, eyes wide with terror.

Then Mike Howerton and the other boys grabbed their friend's arms and pulled him away from the edge. As Howerton recalled years later, the boys "helped him up, shaken from a near-death experience that he would never forget and that I would forever exploit for a sermon illustration." The moral of the story, Howerton concluded, is that cliff jumping—like so many choices we face in life—"requires an *all in* commitment." You are either "all in" or "all out." If you choose to jump off the cliff and you commit to that choice with all your might, you'll be okay. And if you choose not to jump off the cliff and you stick to that decision, you'll be okay. But if you make a halfhearted decision, with the possibility of changing your mind at any point, you stand a very good chance of ending up on the rocks. [26]

The word *decision* comes from the Latin *decidere*, which means "to cut off," from *de-* and *caedere* ("to cut"). Once you make a decision to go in one direction, you cut off all other options and possibilities. If you decide to marry *this* person, you cut off the option of marrying anyone else. If you decide to go to a Chinese restaurant for dinner, you cut off the options of having pizza, boeuf bourguignon, or Kentucky Fried Chicken. Until we grasp what it means to cut off all other options, we don't fully understand what it means to decide.

And because people are often unclear on what a *decision* really is, many people who say they have "made a decision for Christ" actually live like unregenerate pagans. When a person genuinely makes a *decision* for Christ, that person is saying, "I have received Jesus Christ as my Savior and my Lord. I will obey him alone. I willingly relinquish all other options for my life. I choose to completely and finally cut myself off from any possibility of serving false gods. I will serve and obey Jesus alone as the Lord of my life."

One of the identifying characteristics of our postmodern, post-Christian culture is indecision. Many people today refuse to accept that life is made up of either/or decisions. They say, "Why must I choose? Why can't I have it all?" Today's generation wants to keep all options open. They are commitment-phobic. They consider an all-inclusive tolerance to be a virtue, and they reject the notion that some actions, attitudes, and beliefs deserve to be excluded. So they try to keep one foot in each camp, never firmly choosing sides on any issue.

When people are afraid to make decisions and commitments, they end up allowing other people to make their decisions for them. The story is told of a paratrooper who was once asked, "How many jumps have you made?" He replied, "Twenty-five." Then he added, "Actually, I made only one jump. The other twenty-four, I was pushed." You cannot claim to have made a decision when someone else made the decision for you.

We must learn that to decide is to cut off all other options. A key step in spiritual maturity is developing the ability to make firm, righteous decisions—and to commit ourselves 100 percent to keeping those decisions.

Another Cycle of Failure

The English Methodist preacher William Booth founded the Salvation Army in 1865. He is a hero and role model to me, not only because of the ministry he founded, but because of the legacy of faith he passed along to each of his nine children.

One of those children was Marian "Marie" Booth, the third daughter of William and Catherine Booth. Marie suffered an accident early in her life that caused her to have frequent convulsions. Though she was disabled, Marie was intelligent, gracious, and possessed a beautiful Christian spirit. She achieved the rank of staff captain in the Salvation Army.

On one occasion, one of Marie's friends visited her and commiserated with her about her disability. "I don't know why God would allow this to happen to you," the friend said. "You are so intelligent and gifted, and you have such a compassionate heart. Why would God allow you to suffer and live the life of an invalid?"

"It's wonderful to do the Lord's work," Marie replied. "But it is far greater to do the Lord's will." What an amazing statement of trusting, obedient faith. As Christians, we all want to do God's work—but how many of us are truly willing to do God's will, no matter what the personal price?

The book of Judges introduces us to a great woman of God, a prophetess by the name of Deborah, who delivers Israel by making a decision and a commitment to do God's will. We will also meet a weak, indecisive, uncommitted man named Barak. We will learn a lot about the nature of the Christian life and Christian commitment by comparing the deeds of Deborah and Barak.

At this point in the book of Judges, Israel has gone through a time of war against the various Canaanite tribes. Judges 3 opens with the Israelites disobeying God by living among the Canaanites, intermarrying with them, and corrupting themselves by worshiping the Canaanite gods. Each time the Israelites forgot God, each time they slipped into spiritual amnesia, God shook them awake by allowing a pagan nation to oppress them.

After the Israelites had lived in servitude for eight years under the Mesopotamian king Cushan-rishathaim, God raised up a deliverer, the judge Othniel, to lead Israel in a war of liberation. Othniel brought Israel peace and rest for forty years. But then the people again forgot God, and he allowed them to suffer defeat and serve

Eglon, king of Moab, for eighteen years. The people cried out to God for deliverance, and God raised up Ehud, who assassinated Eglon and delivered Israel. After that, the land of Israel had rest for eighty years. After Ehud, God raised up the deliverer Shamgar, who saved Israel by killing six hundred Philistines with a farm implement.

Now, in Judges 4, we meet Deborah and Barak. The chapter opens at the beginning of yet another cycle of failure on the part of Israel. This cycle always begins with failure and disobedience, followed by judgment and oppression, which is then followed by repentance and deliverance. First, let's meet Israel's oppressor:

> And the people of Israel again did what was evil in the sight of the LORD after Ehud died. And the LORD sold them into the hand of Jabin king of Canaan, who reigned in Hazor. The commander of his army was Sisera, who lived in Harosheth-hagoyim. Then the people of Israel cried out to the LORD for help, for he had 900 chariots of iron and he oppressed the people of Israel cruelly for twenty years (4:1-3).

After the death of the judge Ehud, the people of Israel became apathetic and careless. They began to compromise with their Canaanite enemies in a way that was reckless and foolish. They didn't merely allow the Canaanites to move into their neighborhoods. They actually allowed the Canaanites to come in and set up a military camp inside their territory.

A Time for Decision

Next, we meet the deliverer named Deborah:

> Now Deborah, a prophetess, the wife of Lappidoth, was judging Israel at that time. She used to sit under the

palm of Deborah between Ramah and Bethel in the hill country of Ephraim, and the people of Israel came up to her for judgment. She sent and summoned Barak the son of Abinoam from Kedesh-naphtali and said to him, "Has not the LORD, the God of Israel, commanded you, 'Go, gather your men at Mount Tabor, taking 10,000 from the people of Naphtali and the people of Zebulun. And I will draw out Sisera, the general of Jabin's army, to meet you by the river Kishon with his chariots and his troops, and I will give him into your hand'?" Barak said to her, "If you will go with me, I will go, but if you will not go with me, I will not go." And she said, "I will surely go with you. Nevertheless, the road on which you are going will not lead to your glory, for the LORD will sell Sisera into the hand of a woman." Then Deborah arose and went with Barak to Kedesh. And Barak called out Zebulun and Naphtali to Kedesh. And 10,000 men went up at his heels, and Deborah went up with him (4:4-10).

In the Old Testament, the Canaanites were a symbol of Satan, just as Pharaoh symbolized Satan in Egypt. So in this passage, the army of Jabin, king of Canaan, moves into Israel with nine hundred chariots of iron and oppresses Israel cruelly for twenty years. The Canaanites had moved in an inch at a time until they had taken over.

That's how Satan moves into your life and mine—gradually, inch by inch. He's much too subtle for a massive frontal attack. He doesn't want to alarm us so that we will raise our defenses. He doesn't even want us to be aware of his presence. Satan is patient and insidious, and by the time we have awakened to his schemes, it's far too late. Allowing Satan to establish a beachhead in a church, a Christian family, or a Christian life is a recipe for disaster.

The Canaanites simply moved in next-door to Naphtali and

Zebulun, and they gradually became more populous and more powerful. They quietly manufactured hundreds of iron chariots. Perhaps
a day came when the Israelites wondered, "What do the Canaanites need all those chariots for? What do they have in mind?" By the
time the Israelites realized they had a problem, the Canaanites were
too powerful to resist, and for twenty years the Canaanite leader
Sisera used his military might to oppress the people of God.

Likewise Satan is a cruel oppressor once he has wormed his way
into the believer's life. Like Israel in the time of Deborah, we must
shake ourselves awake and realize that we have shunted God aside
and moved him out to the periphery. We have to make a decision.
We have to cut off all other options. We have to say, "Lord, I choose
to place you in control of my life once more. I commit myself to
you to the exclusion of all else. Be the Lord of my life once again."

If ever there has been a time for decision, for total commitment,
and for rejecting compromise, it is now. If ever there has been a time
for parents to unite in prayer, for believers to reject mediocrity, and
for the church to pay the price of authentic discipleship, it is now. If
ever there has been a time for us to choose worship of the Creator
and reject worship of the creation, it is now. If ever there has been
a time to embrace each other and stop fighting one another in the
church, it is now.

If we think there is peace and safety in doing nothing and saying nothing, the next generation will pay the penalty of our silence
and indecision. Unfortunately, many parents are so eager to be liked
by their children, to be buddies to their children, that they never
challenge their children's thinking, never discipline them, and never
guide them to the truth. As Christian parents, we must no longer
be silent. We must cry out to God for the minds and souls of our
children.

In this passage, we see that when the people of Israel were oppressed by the satanic Canaanite military commander Sisera, they cried out to the Lord for help and deliverance. And the Lord heard their cries. He took pity on their suffering. And he raised up a deliverer, Deborah the judge.

Godly Women and Wimpy Men

Deborah was a prophetess, a counselor known for her wisdom. She sat under a palm tree in the hill country of Ephraim, and people would come from miles around, seeking answers to their problems and settlements for their disputes. When Deborah described herself in Judges 5:7, she did not call herself by an exalted title. She simply and humbly said, "I, Deborah, arose as a mother in Israel."

I want you to know that there is no more exalted title than "mother." She could have called herself "Deborah the Judge" or "Deborah the Deliverer"—but neither of these titles would have deserved more honor and respect than "a mother in Israel."

Deborah is one of the most remarkable women in the Bible, and she plays an unusual role in Bible history. It's important that we understand why God raised up Deborah to be a judge in Israel. According to the traditions and values of Hebrew culture at that time, when a woman rose up to lead the nation, it was God's way of shaming the men of that nation. It was God's way of saying to the men, "You have abdicated your leadership responsibility. You have abandoned your role as leaders."

The men of Israel had wimped out on God. So God, in order to humiliate the men, placed courageous Deborah in charge over them. We see this principle expressed in Isaiah 3:12, where God says,

> My people—infants are their oppressors,
>   and women rule over them.

> O my people, your guides mislead you
>   and they have swallowed up the course of your paths.

When God gave Israel a woman to be their judge and deliverer, it was his way of saying, "You are a bunch of children." There are other examples in history when God raised up strong, godly women to fill the gap left by wimpy, ineffectual men.

One of the most significant women in history was Susanna Wesley, the mother of John and Charles Wesley, the cofounders of the Methodist movement. Actress and historian Susan Pellowe (who has often portrayed Susanna Wesley on the stage) writes, "Although she never preached a sermon or published a book or founded a church, [Susanna Wesley] is known as the Mother of Methodism. Why? Because two of her sons, John Wesley and Charles Wesley, as children consciously or unconsciously will, applied the example and teachings and circumstances of their home life."[27]

Susanna Wesley was married to a clergyman, Samuel Wesley, who was a poor provider and was twice jailed for failing to meet his financial obligations. Susanna gave birth to nineteen children, nine of whom died in infancy. She homeschooled the rest. Once, Samuel and Susanna had a minor dispute, and Samuel walked out on her and the children for more than a year. On another occasion, Samuel was away for weeks in London, and another man preached in his place. Sunday after Sunday, the man preached about nothing but repaying one's debts. So Susanna held "church" services in her home with her children, singing songs and reading from the Scriptures. Soon, local church members stopped attending the church and began attending Susanna's home Bible study. Susanna Wesley was an eighteenth-century Deborah, raised up by God to fill the gap left by her weak and ineffectual husband.

When the Lord's disciples fled from him, who stood by him at the foot of the cross? His women followers! Mary, the mother of Jesus was there. So was Mary Magdalene, the woman who loved him greatly because she had been forgiven so much. Salome, the mother of James and John, also stood by as Jesus hung on the cross. These women remained at the Lord's side, comforting him and filling the gap left by the defection of his frightened and dispirited disciples.

In Judges 4, God raises up Deborah to fill the gap left by the weak and ineffectual Barak. We see God speaking through Deborah to Barak in verses 6 and 7, as she says to him, "Has not the LORD, the God of Israel, commanded you, 'Go, gather your men at Mount Tabor, taking 10,000 from the people of Naphtali and the people of Zebulun. And I will draw out Sisera, the general of Jabin's army, to meet you by the river Kishon with his chariots and his troops, and I will give him into your hand'?"

The name Barak means "lightning"—but he is neither as bright nor as quick as lightning. Deborah must remind him that God has commanded him to gather his army. It wasn't a suggestion or a request. God *commanded* Barak. The message could not have been clearer. All Barak needed to do was obey. He simply needed to follow directions. But you know what they say about men and directions! Barak could not bring himself to do what God had commanded him to do.

Now notice the character of Deborah. She is bold and courageous—but she is not ambitious for her own glory. She knows that Barak has a God-given role to play, even though he refuses to fill it. She will not usurp Barak's role as commander, even though she easily could. She will not go beyond God's call upon her life. Instead, she tries to convince Barak to man up and start acting like a soldier of the Lord. She doesn't want to dominate Barak or seize power for herself. She's not a control freak, nor does she lust after power and glory. She simply wants God's will to be done.

Deborah is content to be God's mouthpiece, God's chosen messenger. She is willing to communicate to Barak and deliver to him God's divine strategy for victory—and she fulfills her role perfectly.

A Generation Lost

It was bedtime for a little boy, and his mother tucked him in, listened to his prayers, then left him to fall asleep. Outside, a storm raged. Lightning flashed and thunder rattled the boy's bedroom window. Frightened, he called to his mother. She came in and comforted him for a while, then got up to leave.

"Don't go!" the little boy pleaded. "I'm afraid of the thunder!"

"But honey," the mother replied, "I have to go now and stay with Daddy."

"Why? Is Daddy afraid of the thunder too?"

The notion of a grown man being afraid of thunder seems silly—but no more ridiculous than the behavior of Barak in Judges 4. God has given him a divine strategy and a divine promise of victory—"I will give him into your hand." But Barak is like that scared little boy who cowers under his covers at the sound of thunder. He says to Deborah, "If you will go with me, I will go, but if you will not go with me, I will not go." In other words, "I won't go into battle without my mommy."

No wonder Israel was in trouble! If the head of Israel's army was afraid of his own shadow, imagine the condition of the rest of the army. Barak had no trust in the promises of God, so he refused to obey God. The only confidence he had was in a woman, Deborah the prophetess.

Only by believing the promises of God can we truly obey God.

Barak's failure of nerve was, at its base, a failure of faith and obedience. When God promised to deliver Israel, Barak should have
believed God. He should have gone straight to the battlefield with
full confidence in God's sovereign plan. A believer who truly believes
God's promises can go forth in power, faith, and obedience.

The flaw in Barak's character was that he thought he could offer
partial obedience, conditional obedience, to God. Anything less
than full obedience will rob you of blessing and victory. Partial obedience is an affront to a holy God. It's as if we are saying, "I don't
know if I can trust you, God. I need additional assurances. I need to
protect myself in case your promises fail. I need a little extra insur-
ance and maybe an escape route or two—just in case you don't come
through for me." We miss out on God's blessing for our lives when
we set conditions on our obedience.

You can hear the disgust in Deborah's voice as she answers him.
She is offended by his weakness and lack of faith, but she will do the
best she can with the paltry faith and limited obedience Barak offers
her. She replies, "I will surely go with you. Nevertheless, the road on
which you are going will not lead to your glory, for the LORD will
sell Sisera into the hand of a woman." In other words, "Fine, I'll go
with you under your conditions, but you are going to lose the blessing and the honor that goes with unconditional obedience to God.
You had an opportunity to win honor and glory through obedience
to God. But since this is your response, you will receive dishonor
instead. God will send a woman to do your job."

Deborah knew she was God's rebuke to the faithlessness of Israel.
She also knew that a sovereign God would accomplish his purpose—
with or without the obedience of Barak. As Ephesians 1:11 tells us,
God "works all things according to the counsel of his will." If we
have confidence in his will and we eagerly obey his will, we will

receive an unimaginable blessing from him. But if we hold back, if we set conditions, if we offer only reluctant and partial obedience to his commands, we will miss out on the blessing. God will accomplish his purpose, but we will be left out of the victory celebration.

When God speaks to you and offers you a role in carrying out his eternal plan, you have a choice. You can obey, fully and instantly. You can disobey and rebel against God. Or you can take the path of Barak—you can set conditions on your obedience. You can say, "God, I'll go along with you on this, but you have to do it my way." And partial obedience is not obedience at all. Obedience is all or nothing.

People cannot hinder the will of God. He always accomplishes his purpose. If we refuse to cooperate, then God simply says, "Okay, I'll go around you. I'll work through someone else and let that person have the blessing. I'll let that person share in the victory celebration. You will miss out."

Let me ask you: How do you view your church? Is your church a place you attend as a spectator? Do you go there each week to hear a message, to hear good music, and to be inspired? Or is your church a boot camp and a field headquarters for spiritual warfare? Do you go to church to be outfitted and equipped for the spiritual battles you face throughout the week? Are you a spectator—or are you a soldier?

Spectator Christians have not discovered God's true purpose for placing them in the church, the body of Christ. God never intended for his church to be an arena filled with spectators. A church that is nothing more than an audience of spectators actually poses a danger to the next generation because that church is a place of mass disobedience to God's will.

When Jesus announced his vision of the church in Matthew 16:18, he pictured the church as an army, a fighting force on the move, an invasion force taking territory all the way to the gates of hell—"and the gates of hell," he said, "shall not prevail against it." When Christians lose sight of the Lord's vision for the church, when they begin to see themselves as passive members of an audience and the church as a form of passive entertainment, spiritual amnesia sets in. When parents fail to grasp the true purpose of the church of Jesus Christ, they leave a legacy of ignorance, powerlessness, and faithlessness to their children. Future generations will pay the price for the disobedience of their parents and grandparents.

Evangelical author Josh McDowell cites the shocking results of research by the Josephson Institute of Ethics. Their study of teens who claim they have "accepted Christ" found that 74 percent cheat on school tests, 83 percent lie to their teachers, 93 percent lie to their parents, and 63 percent have behaved with physical violence toward others when angry. These are *self-described Christian teens*—yet their behavior is no more than 4 percentage points different from that of teens who profess no Christian faith at all.

McDowell also cites research he commissioned by the Barna Research Group. Barna found that, of today's self-described Christian teens, 64 percent believe that "if a person is generally good or does enough good things for others during their life, they will earn a place in heaven." Other findings: 63 percent of "Christian" teens don't believe Jesus is the Son of God, 58 percent believe that all religions teach equally valued truths, 51 percent don't believe in the resurrection of Jesus, 65 percent don't believe in the reality of Satan, 68 percent don't believe the Holy Spirit actually exists, and 70 percent don't believe in the existence of absolute moral truth.[28]

This is a statistical snapshot of an entire generation in the grip of spiritual amnesia. How has this happened? How have we lost the vast majority of young people in our church so that their worldview and their faith are indistinguishable from paganism? Have we parents been too busy, too involved in our careers and even our church work to truly engage with our children and find out what they are thinking? These facts should frighten us and make us weep. I hope they will shake us out of our stupor and motivate us to action.

The Deborahs in Our Midst

Even though there is much to lament in the church today, there is also much to be thankful for. There are many Deborahs in our midst—faithful women who obey the Lord without hesitation, who do not stop at partial obedience, who do not keep one foot in the world and one foot in God's will. They are all in. They are 100 percent committed. They are instantly obedient to whatever God calls them to do.

And I hurt for those Deborahs in our midst who must endure the heartache and frustration of living with wimpy Christian men who will not lead. I honestly felt a deep pain in my chest as I read the story of Deborah in the book of Judges. To me, this is not just an ancient story in an ancient book. Deborah's story parallels the stories of many twenty-first-century women in the church who are dealing with men like Barak and are longing for men to step up and lead, but to no avail.

It is the will of God for us to be found faithful. It is the will of God for us to be trusting and obedient. Remember the words of the prophet Samuel to King Saul: "Behold, to obey is better than sacrifice, and to listen than the fat of rams" (1 Samuel 15:22). Many are sacrificing but few are obeying. Many are busy with religious activities but few trust God enough to dare great things for him. Many fill the spectator seats on Sunday mornings but few cry out to the Lord for their children, for themselves, for their church, and for their nation.

In Israel, the people suffered under the oppressor until conditions became so intolerable that the people cried out to the Lord—and God raised up their deliverer. Cry out to the Lord, and he will hear you and deliver you.

Next, we come to the battle between God's people, Israel, and Satan's people, the Canaanites:

> Now Heber the Kenite had separated from the Kenites, the descendants of Hobab the father-in-law of Moses, and had pitched his tent as far away as the oak in Zaanannim, which is near Kedesh.
>
> When Sisera was told that Barak the son of Abinoam had gone up to Mount Tabor, Sisera called out all his chariots, 900 chariots of iron, and all the men who were with him, from Harosheth-hagoyim to the river Kishon. And Deborah said to Barak, "Up! For this is the day in which the LORD has given Sisera into your hand. Does not the LORD go out before you?" So Barak went down from Mount Tabor with 10,000 men following him. And the LORD routed Sisera and all his chariots and all his army before Barak by the edge of the sword. And Sisera got down from his chariot and fled away on foot. And Barak pursued the chariots and the army to Harosheth-hagoyim, and all the army of Sisera fell by the edge of the sword; not a man was left.
>
> But Sisera fled away on foot to the tent of Jael, the wife of Heber the Kenite, for there was peace between Jabin the king of Hazor and the house of Heber the Kenite. And Jael came out to meet Sisera and said to him, "Turn aside, my lord; turn aside to me; do not be afraid." So he turned aside to her into the tent, and she covered him

with a rug. And he said to her, "Please give me a little water to drink, for I am thirsty." So she opened a skin of milk and gave him a drink and covered him. And he said to her, "Stand at the opening of the tent, and if any man comes and asks you, 'Is anyone here?' say, 'No.'" But Jael the wife of Heber took a tent peg, and took a hammer in her hand. Then she went softly to him and drove the peg into his temple until it went down into the ground while he was lying fast asleep from weariness. So he died. And behold, as Barak was pursuing Sisera, Jael went out to meet him and said to him, "Come, and I will show you the man whom you are seeking." So he went in to her tent, and there lay Sisera dead, with the tent peg in his temple.

So on that day God subdued Jabin the king of Canaan before the people of Israel. And the hand of the people of Israel pressed harder and harder against Jabin the king of Canaan, until they destroyed Jabin king of Canaan (Judges 4:11-24).

Even when Barak finally went to the battlefield with Deborah alongside him, Deborah had to prod him to lead. "Up!" she said. "For this is the day in which the Lord has given Sisera into your hand. Does not the Lord go out before you?"

Deborah's frustration with Barak reminds me of a conversation I had some years ago. A faithful, godly woman told me she struggled with her husband's lack of spiritual leadership. Finally, she looked at me with exasperation and said, "Michael, I just can't follow a parked car." And that's what Deborah was dealing with in Barak. It was time for him to get up and lead, yet he was stuck in park.

Prodded by Deborah, Barak finally took his force of ten thousand men and went to war against the army of Sisera. Verses 15 and 16 tell us that "the LORD routed Sisera and all his chariots and all his army…Barak pursued the chariots and the army to Harosheth-hagoyim, and all the army of Sisera fell by the edge of the sword; not a man was left."

The only Canaanite survivor was Sisera himself, who abandoned his chariot and fled the battlefield on foot. He went to the tent of Heber the Kenite, whose household was at peace with Jabin, the king of the Canaanites. Heber's wife, Jael, showed him hospitality, giving him milk to drink, covering him with a blanket, and agreeing to hide him there. Yet her sympathies were with the Israelites.

As Sisera slept, she went quietly to him with a hammer in one hand and a tent peg in the other. With all the force she could summon, she slammed the tent peg with the hammer, driving it into Sisera's temple. She literally nailed his head to the ground. When Barak and his fellow soldiers arrived, searching for Sisera, Jael met them and told them, "Come, and I will show you the man whom you are seeking." And she led them to the corpse of Sisera, still fastened to the ground.

The prophecy of Deborah was fulfilled, as she had spoken it to Barak: "The road on which you are going will not lead to your glory, for the LORD will sell Sisera into the hand of a woman" (4:9). God delivered his people from the satanic menace of Sisera and the Canaanites—and all the credit for the victory went to two women, Deborah and Jael. Though it was Barak's job as captain of the army to wield the sword and destroy the enemy, he missed out on God's blessing because he would not trust and obey. He would not make an "all in" decision and commit himself 100 percent. He left the decision to others.

What is the lesson of this story for your life? You may see yourself as decisive by nature and say, "I could never wimp out like Barak." But consider this: Barak wasn't always a wimp. No one rises to a position of leadership as head of the army by being a wimp. I don't believe Barak lacked courage. I'm convinced he lacked only one thing: faith. He was unwilling to believe God and trust God and act on his promises. And that is why Barak—a man who had undoubtedly demonstrated courage and skill on the battlefield many times in the past—wimped out when God commanded him to take on Sisera and the Canaanites. Trusting in your own human courage will undoubtedly carry you for a while, but eventually human courage fails. That's when you need faith, commitment, and obedience to pick up where human courage leaves off.

You may see yourself as weak and indecisive by nature. You may say, "I could never demonstrate the faith and boldness of Deborah. I could never be a leader." Nonsense. Of course you can be a leader. God wants every believer to be a leader. All you have to do is to believe God's promises and obey him. Christian leadership is simply obedience, nothing more, nothing less. If you obey God, you are a leader by definition, and you will stand head and shoulders above most of your generation. Any person of faith is a leader by example.

If you obey God, you will find yourself in conflict with other people. Leaders are often the target of criticism, opposition, and ridicule. Don't let the opposition of others trouble you in the least. That's the Lord's problem, not yours. Your only problem is deciding how you will obey him today and then committing yourself 100 percent to that course of action. As long as you know you are doing God's will, there's no need to second-guess yourself or defend your actions to critics. Simply keep moving forward, trusting and obeying. People will disapprove, and they may even be offended, but that doesn't make you wrong; it makes you a leader.

The Song of Deborah

Judges 5 is a song Deborah herself probably wrote, praising God for his deliverance. This song contains some important information. It tells us, for example, how terrible the conditions were during the oppression by the Canaanites:

> "In the days of Shamgar, son of Anath,
>   in the days of Jael, the highways were abandoned,
>   and travelers kept to the byways.
> The villagers ceased in Israel;
>   they ceased to be until I arose;
>   I, Deborah, arose as a mother in Israel."
>   (5:6-7)

The Canaanites maintained a reign of terror so frightful that no one dared to go out on the highways for fear of being robbed and killed. The Canaanite terrorists kept God's people in the grip of fear. The Israelites had no strength to resist the Canaanite oppression. They were so demoralized they didn't even dare make weapons to defend themselves. Why had this oppression come upon God's people? We read:

> "When new gods were chosen,
>   then war was in the gates.
> Was shield or spear to be seen
>   among forty thousand in Israel?"
>   (5:8)

God's people chose new gods for themselves to worship. They didn't abandon Yahweh altogether. But they added new gods, Canaanite idols, to their worship of Yahweh. Are we any different? We worship the Lord, we go to church every Sunday, yet we also worship idols of materialism, financial security, social position, ambition, pleasure, and power.

In order to lead in our culture, we have to make a decision, and we have to commit ourselves to that decision. We have to put away our idols. We have to serve God and God alone. If we do that, we will be leaders and deliverers. If we fail to do that, we will be wimps like Barak, and our children and children's children will pay the price.

As my children were growing up, I often told them, "Somebody has to lead. It might as well be you." And I have the same message for you today: be the leader. Why let unbelievers lead you? You lead them! Be the leader in your school, be the leader in your workplace, be the leader wherever you are. Lead for Christ. Lead as an example. Lead in your home. Lead in society. God is looking to raise up a leader, and it might as well be you.

Don't be a wimp like Barak. Wimps are afraid to lead because they know that leaders become targets for criticism and opposition. Wimps want to be spectators not leaders. Wimps want to blend into society not stand out from it.

Don't be a wimp. Be a leader. Step up. Stand out. Believe God. Obey him.

Maybe you're a young person, and you say, "My parents didn't set an example of faith, obedience, and spiritual leadership. My parents let me down." Perhaps that's true—but that's no reason for you to let the next generation down. Even if your elders missed out on the revival, you can obey God. You can become a leader in your generation. You can become the man Barak should have been or the woman that Deborah was. You can be a leader.

The song of Deborah ends with these words:

"So may all your enemies perish, O LORD!
But your friends be like the sun as he rises in his might."
(5:31a)

And Judges 5 ends with this statement of the result of God's victory over Sisera and the Canaanite enemy: "And the land had rest for forty years" (5:31b).

So make a decision—a firm and final decision. No waffling, no going back. Choose today to obey God and trust his promises. Cry out to God. Ask him to transform you into a leader who will impact the world for Christ and who will influence generations to come. Ask him to replace your agenda with his agenda, your selfish ambition with godly ambition, your weakness with his strength, your timidity with his confidence.

Be a friend of God and shine like the sun.

4

God Always
Keeps His Promises

George Müller (1805–1898) was an evangelist and director of the Ashley Down Orphanage in England. Over his lifetime, he cared for more than 10,000 orphans. He also founded scores of schools offering a Bible-based education to more than 120,000 children, including many orphans. Evangelist R.A. Torrey called Müller "one of the mightiest men of prayer" of his generation.

Müller lived by a firm rule that he would never ask anyone for money to support his ministry and would not even mention the needs of the orphanage to another person. Müller was 100 percent committed to trusting fully in God. Even when there was no money to buy milk for the orphans, Müller kept the need between himself and God alone—and God never let him down. Over his ministry career, Müller saw God bring in more than $7 million through prayer alone.

R.A. Torrey wrote that whenever George Müller felt a burden to pray for a specific need, "he would search the Scriptures to find if there was some promise that covered the case. Sometimes he would search the Scriptures for days before he presented his petition to God. And then when he found the promise, with his open Bible before him, and his finger upon that promise, he would plead that promise, and so he received what he asked. He always prayed with an open Bible before him."[29]

Throughout his ministry, George Müller proved again and again that God always keeps his promises. Müller searched the Scriptures for God's promises, he kept his Bible open to those promises, and he prayed those promises—and God never failed him.

One of the great promises of Scripture is found in the book of Proverbs:

> Trust in the LORD with all your heart,
>   and do not lean on your own understanding.
> In all your ways acknowledge him,
>   and he will make straight your paths.
>   (Proverbs 3:5-6)

One of the questions people ask most often is, "What is the will of God for my life? How can I discover God's will for me?" This question takes on extra urgency at the decision points in life, when we have to decide which college to attend, which job offer to accept, whether to propose marriage (or accept a proposal), whether to have children, whether to pursue full-time Christian ministry, and so forth.

We want to trust the Lord, not our own understanding, and we want God to make our paths straight, but we don't know how to discern the will of God. I've talked to people who say, "When I'm not sure what God wants me to do, I just close my eyes, open my Bible, and place my finger blindly on the page. Then I read the verse my finger touched and do whatever it tells me."

When I ask if that has been a reliable guide to decision-making, they invariably admit it has not. In fact, a story is told of a man who tried this questionable method of seeking guidance from Scripture. He was despondent about his financial difficulties, so he shut his eyes, opened his Bible, and plunked his finger down on Matthew 27:5. He read that Judas "went and hanged himself." Horrified, he tried it again and his finger landed on Luke 10:37 and the words, "Go, and do likewise." Even worse! So he tried again, and this time his finger landed on John 13:27 and the words, "What you are going to do, do quickly."

If we want to know God's will for our lives, we need to search the Scriptures. But we need to search the Scriptures with our eyes open, not closed.

In Judges 6, we see the people of Israel once again fall away from God—and God must reawaken the people to their need for him. Following the forty years of peace Israel enjoyed after being delivered by Deborah, the Israelites again do evil in the sight of the Lord, and the Lord allows the Midianites to oppress them. But God is merciful, and he calls another judge, a deliverer named Gideon. As we shall see, Gideon has an unusual way of seeking God's will for his life.

Four Misconceptions

Over the years, I have encountered many people who have misconceptions about the will of God. I have found that these misconceptions fall into four basic categories.

First misconception: "If I accept God's will for my life, I will have to endure pain and suffering."

Let's be clear: pain and suffering are an inescapable part of the human condition. Everyone goes through trials, setbacks, opposition, illness, loss, and sorrow. No one escapes. The only place where there is no pain, where there are no tears, is heaven. So whether you accept God's will for your life or reject it, you can expect times of suffering.

And let's also be clear on this: God loves to give good gifts to his children. The idea that God's will for our lives is a lifetime of pain and suffering has no basis in Scripture. Where does this idea come from? The only place this notion could *possibly* come from is the whispering, lying voice of Satan. Don't listen to his lies. Listen to the assurance of the Word of God: "Or which one of you, if his son asks him for bread, will give him a stone? Or if he asks for a fish, will give him a serpent? If you then, who are evil, know how to give good gifts to your children, how much more will your Father who is in heaven give good things to those who ask him!" (Matthew 7:9-11; see also Psalm 119:165; John 4:10; Romans 5:8; 2 Corinthians 9:15; James 1:17; and Revelation 22:17).

Second misconception: "If I am suffering, I must be outside of God's will."

Many Christians who are already going through a difficult time will actually torment themselves and add to their suffering, thinking that the trial they are going through is a punishment from God or a consequence of being outside of God's will—yet they can't think of any reason why they are being punished.

It's true that God will sometimes allow trials in our lives in order to awaken us and turn our attention back to him. But when that happens, the person who suffers is always aware that there is a sin in his or her life. When God disciplines us, we know the reason why.

If our hearts are right with God, if we are seeking to be humble, responsive, and obedient to his leading, and we suddenly find ourselves going through a time of trial, then we will simply need to endure that trial, clinging to God for dear life while asking him to increase our maturity, faith, and character through that experience. Very often, suffering comes into our lives *precisely because we are living a righteous and obedient life*. As the apostle Paul told Timothy, "Indeed, all who desire to live a godly life in Christ Jesus will be persecuted" (2 Timothy 3:12). And the apostle Peter said, "For it is better to suffer for doing good, if that should be God's will, than for doing evil" (1 Peter 3:17).

Third misconception: "Only those who are called to full-time ministry have God's calling upon their lives."

All believers are called by God. He has a plan for every believer's life. Christian pastors, Christian doctors, Christian truck drivers, Christian entrepreneurs, Christian financial planners, Christian soldiers, Christian first responders, Christian educators, Christian plumbers, Christian garbage collectors, Christian lawyers, and Christian stay-at-home moms are all called by God, and they serve him in their callings. There are no second-class citizens in the kingdom of heaven.

Fourth misconception: "You must feel completely and constantly fulfilled in your profession or else you are out of God's will."

Work is honorable and noble, but God did not create us to find our fulfillment in our vocation. Our fulfillment comes from knowing him. It's a great blessing to love the work you do, but even if you are privileged to work at your dream job, your complete fulfillment should come from the Lord Jesus Christ himself, and not from your vocation.

Now that we've put to rest these four misconceptions, let's meet this man named Gideon and see how he seeks to understand God's will for his life.

Gideon is a likable character. He is easy to identify with, and most of us find it easy to put ourselves in Gideon's sandals because he's no super-saint. He exhibits doubts and indecision. He is truly one of us. Yet he is mentioned in the great roll call of faith in Hebrews (see Hebrews 11:32). It gives me hope to know that this doubting and insecure man is listed in the New Testament as a hero of the faith.

Now, before I point the finger of criticism at Gideon, I have to look in the mirror and see that Gideon's fallen nature is also my fallen nature. Before God can use Gideon to deliver his people from the menace of the Midianites, God has to deliver him from his own faithlessness. And God continually has to deliver me as well. Just as God has to empower Gideon to overcome his doubt, God has to continually conquer doubt in my life. Just as God had to release Gideon from his feelings of inadequacy, God has to continually teach me to trust in his adequacy alone.

Judges 6 confronts us with four questions:

1. *Does God ever abandon us?* (Answer: verses 1-13.)

2. *Can I trust God's will for my life?* (Answer: verses 11-24.)

3. *Will God always watch over me? When I feel the heat of battle, will he be there for me when I need him?* (Answer: verses 25-32.)

4. *Will God fulfill his promises to me?* (Answer: verses 33-40.)

Question 1: Does God Ever Abandon Us? (Judges 6:1-13)

We find the answer to this first question in the first thirteen verses of the passage:

The people of Israel did what was evil in the sight of the Lord, and the Lord gave them into the hand of Midian seven years. And the hand of Midian overpowered Israel, and because of Midian the people of Israel made for themselves the dens that are in the mountains and the caves and the strongholds. For whenever the Israelites planted crops, the Midianites and the Amalekites and the people of the East would come up against them. They would encamp against them and devour the produce of the land, as far as Gaza, and leave no sustenance in Israel and no sheep or ox or donkey. For they would come up with their livestock and their tents; they would come like locusts in number—both they and their camels could not be counted—so that they laid waste the land as they came in. And Israel was brought very low because of Midian. And the people of Israel cried out for help to the Lord.

When the people of Israel cried out to the Lord on account of the Midianites, the Lord sent a prophet to the people of Israel. And he said to them, "Thus says the Lord, the God of Israel: I led you up from Egypt and brought you out of the house of slavery. And I delivered you from the hand of the Egyptians and from the hand of all who oppressed you, and drove them out before you and gave you their land. And I said to you, 'I am the Lord your God; you shall not fear the gods of the Amorites in whose land you dwell.' But you have not obeyed my voice."

Now the angel of the Lord came and sat under the terebinth at Ophrah, which belonged to Joash the Abiezrite, while his son Gideon was beating out wheat in the winepress to hide it from the Midianites. And the angel of the LORD appeared to him and said to him, "The LORD is with you, O mighty man of valor." And Gideon said to him, "Please, sir, if the LORD is with us, why then has all this happened to us? And where are all his wonderful deeds that our fathers recounted to us, saying, 'Did not the LORD bring us up from Egypt?' But now the LORD has forsaken us and given us into the hand of Midian" (6:1-13).

The people have fallen away from God, they have come under the oppression of the Midianites, and now they cry out to God for deliverance. So God comes to them in a *theophany*—an appearance of the Lord Jesus Christ prior to his incarnation. Whenever you see a reference to "the angel of the LORD," this angel is actually the Lord Jesus himself. The word *angel* literally means "messenger" or "emissary," and there were occasions in Old Testament times when the messenger or emissary was the Lord himself. We know that the angel depicted in these verses is the Lord because verse 14 specifically identifies the angel as "the LORD"—"And the LORD turned to him and said…"

So, in this scene, the Lord comes to Gideon and calls him to become the deliverer of Israel. But Gideon replies, "Please, sir, if the LORD is with us, why then has all this happened to us? And where are all his wonderful deeds that our fathers recounted to us, saying, 'Did not the LORD bring us up from Egypt?' But now the LORD has forsaken us and given us into the hand of Midian" (6:13).

In other words, Gideon's response to the Lord's call is, "Why bother? God has already abandoned us. He has sold us out to the Midianites. It's hopeless."

Here, Gideon engages in a fallacy common to us all. We tend

to take the mercy, grace, and provision of God for granted. Yet the moment we experience chastening from God because of our sins, the moment we experience the natural consequences of sin, we groan, "Where is God? Why has he forsaken me?"

God's discipline in our lives is a clear indication that he hates sin—and he loves us too much to allow sin to reign in our lives. Jesus said, "I give them eternal life, and they will never perish, and no one will snatch them out of my hand" (John 10:28). You are always in the protective hand of the Lord Jesus. This doesn't mean you'll never undergo chastening for sin, but it does mean he will never forsake you, never abandon you, and never stop loving you.

Obedience to God builds character. Disobedience destroys character. God's love for Israel was too great for him to allow his people to destroy their own character. So God permitted the Midianites to oppress them as a means of disciplining Israel and restoring the nation's character.

The Israelites labored all year in anticipation of harvesting their crops—and just at the time of harvest, the Midianites swarmed upon Israel like a plague of locusts. They seized their crops and live-stock and stole everything in sight. And what did the Israelites do about it? Like frightened rabbits, they scattered and hid in mountain caves and dens.

How should we apply the lessons of the Midianite oppression to our own lives? The crops and livestock represented Israel's future—and it all went up in smoke because of Israel's sin and neglect of God. What represents our future? Clearly, our greatest asset is the next generation. Our children represent our hopes for the future, our greatest human potential. If we do not equip our children with the Word of God, if we do not prepare them for spiritual battle, they will repeat the error of ancient Israel and flee before their enemy.

When the Israelites were harassed by the Midianites, all they could do was run and hide. They left their crops and livestock undefended. They watched their future go up in smoke. It was seven long years before the Israelites humbled themselves before God.

I don't know what it will take in our own land before God's people show up in prayer meetings and cry out to the Lord. I don't know what we are waiting for. Don't we have spiritual eyes to see that the Midianites are plundering our nation today? Don't we have the spiritual understanding to see that we, as parents and grandparents, are failing to set a spiritual example for the next generation? Aren't we running into the hills and hiding in caves while watching the Midianites of our own time turn our future, the souls of our children, into smoke and ashes?

When will we humble ourselves before God? When will we rise up, cry out to God, and take a stand for righteousness and faith? God is teaching us the same lesson he taught Israel in the time of Gideon: He will never abandon us—yet he longs for us to return to him and cry out to him and intercede on behalf of the next generation.

When the people of Israel finally cried out to the Lord, he sent an unnamed prophet to them (6:8), and the prophet reminded them how God had delivered them from the hand of the Egyptian oppressors in the time of Moses. Then the prophet gave the Israelites this message from God: "And I said to you, 'I am the LORD your God; you shall not fear the gods of the Amorites in whose land you dwell.' But you have not obeyed my voice" (6:10). In other words, when the people fled before the Midianites and hid in the mountain caves, they were disobeying God's command. They were fleeing in terror from the false gods of their enemies. Their fear was an act of disobedience.

God does not want his people to serve false gods, nor does he want us to fear them. God intends for his people to live confidently and faithfully as conquerors. And our confidence comes from knowing that God never abandons us.

Question 2: Can I Trust God's Will for My Life? (Judges 6:11-24)

At the same time God sent this prophet to confront Israel's faithlessness and ingratitude, he was also raising up a deliverer for Israel—a man who would deliver the people from the consequences of their sin. He was raising up a man named Gideon.

Now, Gideon was about as unlikely a hero as you can imagine. No one would ever accuse him of overconfidence. Gideon lacked a godly self-image. He was insecure about his tribe, his clan, and even his own place in his family. As we shall see, Gideon expressed feelings of total inadequacy about his qualifications to be a deliverer of Israel.

But God specializes in turning weaklings into heroes. He loves to take inadequate, insecure people and transform them into servants who lead and leaders who serve. God often passes over the strong, the confident, the self-sufficient—the very people you and I would likely select—and he chooses instead the shy ones, the inexperienced ones, the weak and insecure ones.

In 1 Samuel 16, God directed the prophet Samuel to anoint a successor to King Saul and to choose from among the sons of Jesse. And Jesse presented seven of his strong, confident, intelligent, warrior sons—but God told Samuel that he had not chosen any of them. So Samuel asked, "Are all your sons here?" And that's when Jesse mentioned his youngest, a shepherd boy he hadn't even considered as leadership material. But it was David, the unassuming shepherd boy, the young poet, that God had chosen as the next king of Israel.

When Jesus called his twelve disciples, only one of them, Simon
Peter, had the bold, outgoing personality of a natural leader. The
rest of the Twelve were just average joes, some working-class fisher-
men, a doubting pessimist named Thomas, Matthew the tax collec-
tor (a bureaucrat), Simon the zealot (an anti-government radical),
and so forth. Jesus spent three years teaching these men, mentoring
them, delegating his ministry to them, and pouring his life into
them. With the exception of Judas Iscariot, he succeeded in trans-
forming them into a nucleus of leaders who changed the course
of history. Through those disciples, Jesus founded a community
of believers that has expanded around the globe and continues to
expand to this day.

God is in the business of turning common, ordinary human clay
into faithful, bold leaders. God cannot use people who are so self-
confident they have no need of him. He excels at using the weak
and insecure. That's why he chose Gideon, as we see in the story of
Gideon's calling:

> Now the angel of the LORD came and sat under the tere-
> binth at Ophrah, which belonged to Joash the Abiezrite,
> while his son Gideon was beating out wheat in the wine-
> press to hide it from the Midianites. And the angel of
> the LORD appeared to him and said to him, "The LORD
> is with you, O mighty man of valor." And Gideon said
> to him, "Please, sir, if the LORD is with us, why then has
> all this happened to us? And where are all his wonderful
> deeds that our fathers recounted to us, saying, 'Did not
> the LORD bring us up from Egypt?' But now the LORD
> has forsaken us and given us into the hand of Midian."
> And the LORD turned to him and said, "Go in this might
> of yours and save Israel from the hand of Midian; do not

I send you?" And he said to him, "Please, Lord, how can I save Israel? Behold, my clan is the weakest in Manasseh, and I am the least in my father's house." And the LORD said to him, "But I will be with you, and you shall strike the Midianites as one man." And he said to him, "If now I have found favor in your eyes, then show me a sign that it is you who speak with me. Please do not depart from here until I come to you and bring out my present and set it before you." And he said, "I will stay till you return."

So Gideon went into his house and prepared a young goat and unleavened cakes from an ephah of flour. The meat he put in a basket, and the broth he put in a pot, and brought them to him under the terebinth and presented them. And the angel of God said to him, "Take the meat and the unleavened cakes, and put them on this rock, and pour the broth over them." And he did so. Then the angel of the LORD reached out the tip of the staff that was in his hand and touched the meat and the unleavened cakes. And fire sprang up from the rock and consumed the meat and the unleavened cakes. And the angel of the LORD vanished from his sight. Then Gideon perceived that he was the angel of the LORD. And Gideon said, "Alas, O Lord GOD! For now I have seen the angel of the LORD face to face." But the LORD said to him, "Peace be to you. Do not fear; you shall not die." Then Gideon built an altar there to the LORD and called it, The LORD Is Peace. To this day it still stands at Ophrah, which belongs to the Abiezrites (Judges 6:11-24).

When the messenger of the Lord appeared to Gideon, his first words were, "The LORD is with you, O mighty man of valor." I can easily picture Gideon looking around and saying, "Who are you talking to? Surely, you don't mean me!" Gideon lacked every quality that we normally associate with a hero, with a "mighty man of valor." He lacked faith, vision, and courage. He lacked credentials, background, and experience.

When God's messenger arrived at Ophrah and sat in the shade of the terebinth tree, Gideon was hiding out from the Midianites, threshing some wheat in his father's winepress. Gideon planned to hide the wheat from the Midianites so that he and his father would have something to eat. We can tell from Gideon's words that he felt defeated, pessimistic, and powerless. God was pleased to find Gideon in that depleted state, because God can always do something with depleted people.

Can God do anything with you? He can do nothing with you if you feel self-sufficient and self-satisfied. But he can work miracles through you if you feel powerless. If you go to God and say, "Lord, I have nothing to offer but my obedience," then watch out! You will be amazed to see what he can do with you.

What did God mean when he called Gideon a "mighty man of valor"? This is an Old Testament parallel to what Jesus did for Simon Peter in the New Testament. In Matthew 16:18, Jesus looked at his rash, impetuous, unstable follower Simon and said, "And I tell you, you are Peter." The Aramaic word Jesus used was *Cephas*, which means "rock." So Jesus gave Peter a new name, Peter the Rock, and a new vision for his future. Peter wasn't a rock yet. He would fail miserably, and even deny his Lord, sealing his denial with a curse. But ultimately, Peter would become the rocklike leader of the first-century church.

Gideon was no mighty man of valor—not yet. But God saw the potential in this man, so he greeted him as if he were already a great warrior, and in so doing, God gave Gideon a new self-image to live up to. God sees our potential. He sees what we can be, not what we are. He sees what we can accomplish by depending on his resources instead of our own human inadequacy.

If you are a parent, a grandparent, a teacher, a coach, or a mentor, then here is a message you need to impart to the young people within the sphere of your influence: "God sees you as a mighty warrior for him. You can accomplish literally anything if you depend entirely on God's resources."

You may look at a child and see nothing but bad attitudes, behavioral problems, immaturity, laziness, and a bad temper—but you can give that child a new vision of himself, of herself, a vision of limitless potential in reliance upon God's resources. I plead with you, don't discourage your children, your grandchildren, or your students. At the same time, I plead with you not to do what so many worldly parents and educators are doing today—heaping empty praise on children, inflating their arrogance and pride by telling them they have infinite potential in their humanity.

A godly self-image is not, "I can do anything I want to because I have limitless potential." That's a worldly self-image, and it is utterly false. A godly self-image says (along with the apostle Paul), "I can do all things through him who strengthens me" (Philippians 4:13). Nothing is impossible for those who live in obedience and dependence on the power of God.

God chose a weak and frightened man, a man who was hiding from the Midianites, a man who had very little self-esteem and self-confidence—and God gave this man a vision of what he could become: a mighty man of valor. Why did God choose Gideon? He chose this man specifically so that the people of Israel would know that it was the hand of God that delivered them, not human brains or brawn.

After giving Gideon an expanded vision of the mighty warrior he would become, God told Gideon, "Go." He commissioned Gideon with a task. He said, "Go in this might of yours and save Israel from the hand of Midian; do not I send you?" (6:14).

When Gideon said, "The LORD has forsaken us and given us into the hand of Midian," God didn't waste time arguing with him. God gave Gideon a job to do: "Go." God sent Gideon to save Israel from the Midianite oppressors much as he would later send David to save Israel from Goliath and the Philistines. It must have seemed to Gideon that God was sending him on a "mission impossible." But whenever God sends someone to do his work, he equips that person to achieve victory. When God leads, he guides. When he promises, he fulfills.

Gideon's faith was weak. He protested, "Please, Lord, how can I save Israel? Behold, my clan is the weakest in Manasseh, and I am the least in my father's house." Gideon thought that God was sending him out in his own paltry, insignificant strength. So God corrected his misimpression: "I will be with you, and you shall strike the Midianites as one man."

Gideon was still unconvinced. He wanted some assurance that he could trust God's will for his life. "If now I have found favor in your eyes," Gideon said, "then show me a sign that it is you who speak with me. Please do not depart from here until I come to you and bring out my present and set it before you" (6:17-18).

God understands our limitations and the weakness of our faith. He isn't offended when we ask him for confirmation. Just as Jesus graciously offered his wounds to doubting Thomas as proof of his resurrection, God is patient with us, he knows we are dust, and he stands by us as we struggle to trust and believe him.

Nine years after I moved to Atlanta we founded The Church

of The Apostles. I often prayed to God, seeking to discern his will for the church. In my prayers, I often said, *Lord, just show me.* And the Lord would send the most unlikely people and amazing circumstances into my life to show me that we were moving in the right direction. Why did I ask God to show me? Was it because I doubted God's power or his ability to lead us? Not at all! I had faith in God, I wanted to serve him and obey him, and I put no conditions on how I would serve him. I didn't doubt God, but I doubted myself. I asked God to confirm himself to me so that I could make sure I was truly hearing his voice, not following some false impulse of my own flesh.

That is what Gideon does here. "Show me a sign that it is you who speak with me," he says. He wants to make sure he is truly hearing the voice of God and not following some false leading of his own imagination. God is never offended when we seek assurance that the voice we hear is truly his voice. God was not offended when Gideon sought that assurance. Even when Gideon really pushed his luck and asked a second time, God did not get upset with him.

And how does Gideon seek God's confirmation? The text tells us, "So Gideon went into his house and prepared a young goat and unleavened cakes from an ephah of flour. The meat he put in a basket, and the broth he put in a pot, and brought them to him under the terebinth and presented them" (6:19). In other words, Gideon sacrificed. He didn't seek God's confirmation on the cheap. At a time when the Midianites were destroying the crops and stealing the livestock of the Israelites, Gideon offered to God food that was costly and scarce—the meat of a young goat and cakes of unleavened bread.

Gideon placed the sacrifice on the altar—and fire sprang up from the altar and consumed the sacrifice. And the fire that the Lord sent to the altar terrified Gideon. At that point, he realized who he was dealing with. He recognized the messenger as a manifestation of God himself, and he said, "Alas, O Lord GOD! For now I have seen the angel of the LORD face to face" (6:22).

We all want God to confirm his will to us, but how many of us are willing to sacrifice—truly sacrifice—to discover God's will for our lives? Gideon was willing to pay a serious price to discover God's will. And when the fire sprang up, Gideon was terrified—not because he was afraid that God would do him harm, but because he understood the profound seriousness of being face-to-face with the Creator of the universe. At that moment, he immediately called that place Yahweh-shalom, meaning "The LORD is my peace" or "God is my total well-being."

It is not a sin to seek to confirm God's will for your life. In fact, God is pleased when we take his will that seriously.

You can trust God's will for your life because he is your peace, your total well-being. There is always peace, joy, and contentment when you know you are obeying God's will, even if his will leads through a time of suffering. We have peace knowing that God will never abandon us, and we can always trust his will for our lives.

Question 3: Will God Always Watch Over Me? (Judges 6:25-32)

Will God still be with us out on the battlefield? Can we trust him never to leave us in the heat of battle? The answer is found in the next few verses:

> That night the LORD said to him, "Take your father's bull, and the second bull seven years old, and pull down the altar of Baal that your father has, and cut down the Asherah that is beside it and build an altar to the LORD your God on the top of the stronghold here, with stones laid

in due order. Then take the second bull and offer it as a burnt offering with the wood of the Asherah that you shall cut down." So Gideon took ten men of his servants and did as the LORD had told him. But because he was too afraid of his family and the men of the town to do it by day, he did it by night.

When the men of the town rose early in the morning, behold, the altar of Baal was broken down, and the Asherah beside it was cut down, and the second bull was offered on the altar that had been built. And they said to one another, "Who has done this thing?" And after they had searched and inquired, they said, "Gideon the son of Joash has done this thing." Then the men of the town said to Joash, "Bring out your son, that he may die, for he has broken down the altar of Baal and cut down the Asherah beside it." But Joash said to all who stood against him, "Will you contend for Baal? Or will you save him? Whoever contends for him shall be put to death by morning. If he is a god, let him contend for himself, because his altar has been broken down." Therefore on that day Gideon was called Jerubbaal, that is to say, "Let Baal contend against him," because he broke down his altar (Judges 6:25-32).

It's important to remember that Gideon was an ordinary man, not a super-saint. He had probably lived on the same moral and spiritual plane as the rest of the people of Israel. Like all of his neighbors, Gideon had probably moved God out of the center of his life and off to the margins. He hadn't turned against God, he hadn't rebelled against God, but he had moved God off to the side while he focused his attention on other matters. Gideon had probably been so occupied with survival, with trying to raise his crops and livestock without attracting the notice of the Midianites, that he had very little time for God.

Many of us as Christians live that way as well. We like to think we keep Jesus at the center of our homes, but he's really more of a peripheral matter. Our minds are occupied with career issues, paying the bills, saving for our kids' college education, and our social activities. These are the things that occupy our time. These are the line items in our family budget. We like to think we are focused on Jesus, but if we are honest with ourselves, we have to admit that we keep Jesus at the periphery of our lives.

That's how it was in Israel in those days. In fact, we learn in verses 25-27 that Gideon's own Israelite father was actually a priest of the demon-god Baal. God told Gideon to "pull down the altar of Baal that your father has, and cut down the Asherah that is beside it." The ancient Canaanite cultists would often have an altar of Baal next to an Asherah pole—a tree or pole honoring the Sumerian mother-goddess Asherah. Gideon's father did not merely dabble in Canaanite religion, he was high in the priestly hierarchy of the cult.

For Gideon to challenge the cult of Baal by tearing down the altar and the Asherah pole, he had to defy his father, his entire family, his neighbors, and his culture. He had to battle the peer pressure of his entire society. The spiritual and moral condition of Israel was so debased and the people were so knee-deep in compromise that they were not even aware of how far they had drifted into apostasy. They were oblivious to spiritual reality. They had developed a mass spiritual amnesia and had forgotten the blessings they had received from the hand of God through past generations.

It took courage for Gideon to take a stand and deliver Israel. He had to stand boldly and courageously against the moral and spiritual sewage that spewed from his culture. He had to speak bluntly about the corruption of his society. He was at war not only with the pagan Midianites, but he was also at war with the moral and spiritual compromisers of his society, including his own father. So Gideon had to ask himself, *Will God keep watch over me as I battle my own family and my own culture? Will God be with me in the heat of this fight? Will he support me as I begin to pay the price of leadership?*

When God called Gideon to deliver Israel, he told Gideon to begin at home. He commanded Gideon to destroy the altar where his father, Joash, had sacrificed to Baal. You can never be strong in your faith anywhere else if you are not strong at home. If you are not a role model of Christlike character before your family, it is impossible to be a role model of Christlike character in your neighborhood and your workplace.

As our society becomes increasingly hostile to biblical truth—and the hostility of the world is not coming sometime in the future, it is here already—we as Christians will be tested. When testing comes, we must decide whether to stand for Christ—or fail the test of persecution. I say let the chips fall where they may. I will never cease to preach the gospel and the full counsel of God. If I end up in prison, then I shall have a prison ministry. Will God watch over me if I am in prison? You'd better believe it. He stood by Joseph, Daniel, Peter, and Paul in prison, and he still stands by his faithful followers who pay the price of discipleship today.

Does that mean that all believers who are imprisoned for their faith will be released? No. Some of us will be called to suffer martyrdom for our faith. Whether we are free or in prison, whether we live or die, God will not abandon us. He always watches over us as we do his will.

I'm not saying I wish for martyrdom. I enjoy my comfort and freedom as much as you do. But far more important than comfort and freedom are obedience in service to God and the Lord's commendation at the end of this life, "Well done, good and faithful servant. Enter into the joy of your Master."

God gave Gideon a difficult assignment, but God was with him. When Gideon destroyed the altar of Baal that belonged to his father, the people were outraged. These were Israelites, and yet they were incensed that Gideon had destroyed an altar to a foreign god. This is how far Israel had fallen from the faith. Gideon had acted righteously, in accordance with God's commandments—yet his neighbors wanted to kill him for it. But God used Gideon's compromising, backsliding, apostate father to defend Gideon.

There is a lesson here for all of us as believers. If you are a compromising Christian, if you are living with one foot in God's kingdom and the other foot in the world, it's time for you to choose one or the other. You cannot build an altar to God until you tear down the altars of the false gods in your life. Only you know what those false gods may be. If you are honest, God is probably convicting you of some idols in your life right now. He will not share his glory with idols.

Before Gideon could declare war on the Midianites, he had to declare war on Baal. He had to take a stand against the sin of his own father. And if Gideon had compromised his faith by serving Baal, then he also had to declare war on the Baals in his own life. You cannot open the next door until you pass through the first door—and the first door is to remove all the false gods from your life.

We can trust the will of God for our lives. When he sends us out to the battlefield, he goes with us. He will never abandon us in the heat of battle. You have God's Word on that.

Question 4: Will God Fulfill His Promises to Me? (Judges 6:33-40)

Will God keep his Word and fulfill his promises to me? This is a key question we must answer in our own hearts and minds. If we firmly, wholeheartedly believe the answer is yes, then God can use us to achieve the impossible.

God does not look at people the way we look at people. He is not looking for the most courageous person, the most powerful warrior, the best strategic thinker. God is looking for the one who is conscious of his own weakness. He is looking for the one who relies 100 percent on God's power and wisdom, not his own. He is looking for the one who is willing to grow in reliance on God. He is looking for the one who is willing to take God at his Word.

God is looking for men and women, boys and girls, who are completely obedient and available to him. And that is exactly the kind of leader God has found in Gideon:

> Now all the Midianites and the Amalekites and the people of the East came together, and they crossed the Jordan and encamped in the Valley of Jezreel. But the Spirit of the LORD clothed Gideon, and he sounded the trumpet, and the Abiezrites were called out to follow him. And he sent messengers throughout all Manasseh, and they too were called out to follow him. And he sent messengers to Asher, Zebulun, and Naphtali, and they went up to meet them.
>
> Then Gideon said to God, "If you will save Israel by my hand, as you have said, behold, I am laying a fleece of wool on the threshing floor. If there is dew on the fleece alone, and it is dry on all the ground, then I shall know that you will save Israel by my hand, as you have said."

And it was so. When he rose early next morning and squeezed the fleece, he wrung enough dew from the fleece to fill a bowl with water. Then Gideon said to God, "Let not your anger burn against me; let me speak just once more. Please let me test just once more with the fleece. Please let it be dry on the fleece only, and on all the ground let there be dew." And God did so that night; and it was dry on the fleece only, and on all the ground there was dew (Judges 6:33-40).

Verse 34 tells us that "the Spirit of the LORD clothed Gideon." God's Holy Spirit enveloped Gideon like a well-tailored suit. The Spirit came upon Gideon in a powerful, all-encompassing way because God keeps his promises. He will give you resources you never dreamed possible because he keeps his promises. He will guarantee victory to you because he never goes back on his Word.

Laying Out a Fleece

Judges 6 concludes with the scene in which Gideon seeks to discern God's will by laying out a woolen fleece and asking God to confirm his will through the fleece. To this day, many people speak of "laying out a fleece" as a way of making a decision.

A young woman might pray, *Lord, I don't really want to go to the mission field, but if you want me to be a missionary, then have our pastor preach on missions this Sunday and I'll take that as a sign from you.* Or a teenage boy might say, *God, I'm going to call this girl, and if she answers the phone, I'll know you want me to ask her out on a date—but if I get her voicemail, I won't ask her out.*

Is that the right way to discern God's will for our lives? Is that really the pattern Gideon set for us? Although God is patient with Gideon's questions and does not rebuke him for laying out a fleece, there are a number of good reasons for not following Gideon's example.

First, Gideon did not have the indwelling Spirit of God as you and I do. Yes, the Holy Spirit "clothed" Gideon for a limited time (6:34), but Gideon did not have the indwelling Holy Spirit all the time. You and I do not have to put out a "fleece" because we have the Holy Spirit living within us. His wisdom is always available to us. Instead of placing your trust in a fleece, shouldn't you place your trust in the inner guidance of the Holy Spirit? As Jesus himself promised, "When the Spirit of truth comes, he will guide you into all the truth" (John 16:13a).

Second, Gideon did not have the Bible to rely on. God's Word reveals God's will to us in many specific ways. For example, Paul writes, "Rejoice always, pray without ceasing, give thanks in all circumstances; *for this is the will of God in Christ Jesus for you*" (1 Thessalonians 5:16-18). Those verses may not tell you whom you should marry or which car you should buy, but they tell you how to live victoriously, following the will of God. Everything we need to know about discerning God's will is found in God's Word.

Third, Gideon did not have the role model of Jesus to look up to. Because we can examine the life of Jesus and follow the teachings of Jesus, many of life's biggest decisions become easier to make. Paul wrote, "Let the word of Christ dwell in you richly, teaching and admonishing one another in all wisdom, singing psalms and hymns and spiritual songs, with thankfulness in your hearts to God" (Colossians 3:16). Paul also reminds us that "we have the mind of Christ" (1 Corinthians 2:16b). The more we practice the presence of Christ in our lives, the clearer our decisions become.

Fourth, and most important, Gideon *already knew* God's will in this situation. He was not asking God to point him in one direction or another. Gideon was merely asking God to reassure him and confirm that he had rightly interpreted God's leading for his life.

What does God really want to produce in our lives? Does he want us to seek a sign from him for every decision we face, every purchase we make, or every question we ponder? Or does God want us to develop Christlike character and wisdom so that we can make mature and godly decisions without constantly seeking a sign from him? When we pray continually, live joyfully and thankfully, and do everything in the name of Jesus, then our thoughts and our decisions will be aligned with God's will, and he will bless us with his peace. We will no longer feel the need to lay out a fleece or seek a sign from God.

One problem with laying out a fleece is that it limits God to a yes/no, either/or choice. What if God wants to reveal to you a wider range of options? By laying out a fleece, you have limited God. It's also rather presumptuous to go before the Creator of the universe and tell him the exact way that he must answer your request for guidance.

If you are struggling with a difficult question and you want to know God's mind in the matter, there are much richer, deeper ways of seeking his will than laying out a fleece. You can search the Scriptures. You can fast and pray. You can seek counsel and prayer from trusted Christian friends and advisers.

Gideon's fleeces required miraculous, supernatural intervention into the laws of nature. The wet fleece on the dry floor yielded a bowlful of water—and the fleece on the wet floor was dry. These were clearly miraculous occurrences. Yet most of what people today call "laying out a fleece" consists of asking God to speak through ordinary, everyday circumstances that might easily occur by the simple workings of chance: *Lord, if you really want me to do this, let me know by playing my favorite song on the radio.*

Though God wants us to rely on him for strength, he also wants us to grow in Christlike wisdom, discernment, and judgment. That's why the apostle Paul writes, "Look carefully then how you walk, not as unwise but as wise, making the best use of the time, because the days are evil. Therefore do not be foolish, but understand what the will of the Lord is" (Ephesians 5:15-17).

Principles for Discerning God's Will

Finally, let me suggest some basic principles for discerning the will of God when making big decisions. These are the principles I follow whenever I seek to discover God's will for any specific situation.

First, when seeking the mind and will of God, I search my heart and make sure I am living obediently under the lordship of Jesus Christ. I ask myself, *Is every area of my life under his lordship? Am I holding anything back?*

Second, I try to purify my motives and put all my personal desires in neutral. We human beings easily deceive ourselves into thinking that what *we* want is what *God* wants. I don't want to fall in love with a certain pursuit or ambition that would violate God's will for my life. Instead, I want to put my desires in neutral so that God can have his way and work his will in my life.

Third, I go to God in prayer and ask him to speak to me through his Word, through prayer and meditation, through listening to his Spirit, and through the circumstances of my life, including the opening and shutting of doors. It's perfectly legitimate to say to God, *Lord, if you would have me go in this direction, please open the door. And if you would have me not go in this direction, please close the door. Lord, I ask you to make your will clear to me through the circumstances of my life.*

Fourth, test the spirits. The apostle John wrote, "Beloved, do not believe every spirit, but test the spirits to see whether they are from God, for many false prophets have gone out into the world" (1 John 4:1). How do we test the spirits? We subject every decision, every option, every question to a series of tests:

- Is the choice I'm considering going to bring glory to God?

- Will this choice set a good example and be a good witness for Jesus Christ?

- Is this choice consistent with God's Word—or does it violate God's Word?

These simple tests often bring great clarity to the decisions we face.

Fifth and finally, wait upon the Lord. Wait for his timing. And while you are waiting, bathe your mind in God's Word. We don't like to wait, but if we are honest with ourselves, we have to confess that the times we have been wrong about God's will are usually the times we have been hasty and impatient. God is never in a hurry— but Satan is always trying to rush us into decisions before the right time. As the psalmist wrote,

> Be still before the LORD and wait patiently for him;
> fret not yourself over the one who prospers in his way,
> over the man who carries out evil devices!
> (Psalm 37:7)

Waiting is never easy. I remember the two years of waiting from the time I first felt the burden to begin The Church of The Apostles until we actually had our first church service. Anyone who says that waiting is easy is wrong. Waiting for God's timing is very difficult and takes great faith and wisdom. But few experiences in life produce greater wisdom and Christian character than waiting patiently on the Lord.

We have asked four questions, and the story of Gideon has yielded four answers. Now it's time for the quiz, when we check the answers to those questions:

1. *Does God ever abandon us?* No, never!

2. *Can I trust God's will for my life?* Yes, absolutely!

3. *Will God always watch over me?* Yes!

4. *Will God fulfill his promises to me?* Yes, without question.

God called Gideon to be a judge and deliverer of Israel. Next, we will see how Gideon obediently followed God's remarkable plan for delivering Israel from the Midianites.

5

The Budding Faith
of Gideon

A young man once told me, "No matter what I did, I could never please my father. When I cut the grass, I worked my heart out to make it perfect, hoping for a few words of praise. But my dad always found a few blades of grass that I missed. I would clean the garage, get all the tools perfectly arranged, remove all the cobwebs, and sweep the floor as clean as my mother's table. He still found things to complain about.

"Once, I came home from school with my report card—all *A*s except for one *B*. My stomach was in knots when I handed it to him because I knew what would happen, and it did. He spent the whole time demanding to know why that *B* wasn't an *A*. To this day, I see myself as a failure. Sometimes, people tell me I did a good job, but it means nothing to me. I only hear my father's voice, telling me I never do anything right."

This young man became a Christian and was totally committed to living for Christ, yet he struggled to understand the grace of God. He had an image of God as a demanding father, and he believed he could never work hard enough to please the Lord.

I have met many people who were raised by overly demanding parents. People who are raised this way tend to wobble between spiritual highs and spiritual lows. For a while, they can catch a glimpse of God's grace and they feel loved and accepted by God. That's an emotional and spiritual high point—but it never lasts long. Soon, the voice of the demanding, critical parent is heard in the conscience. The person feels like a loser. He crashes emotionally and spiritually.

The children of overly demanding parents tend to obsess over certain verses or phrases in the Bible. A common example is the person who says, "But doesn't the Bible say that it's impossible to please God?"

"You're thinking of Hebrews 11:6," I reply, "but you are misquoting the verse. It says, *And without faith* it is impossible to please him, for whoever would draw near to God must believe that he exists and that he rewards those who seek him.' If you have faith in him, God is pleased. And if you seek him, he will reward you. The same verse that you have been beating yourself down with actually says that God is pleased with your faith in him."

A true understanding of the amazing grace of our loving God is the beginning of the healing process. The false notion of God as a demanding, critical parent who must continually be appeased is at the root of all human-made religions. But the essence of a relationship with Jesus Christ is love, forgiveness, and grace.

When Martin Luther was a young Dominican monk, he was so burdened with a sense of sin and unworthiness that he would go to the abbot of the monastery every hour to make a confession. Finally, the abbot got tired of his confessions and told him not to come back. Luther later recalled, "I lost touch with Christ the Savior and Comforter, and made of him the jailor and hangman of my poor soul."[30]

One day, Luther opened the Word of God and read, "The righteous shall live by faith" (Romans 1:17). The light of truth shone on Luther's troubled soul. In a flash of realization, he understood that salvation is by grace through faith and not a matter of our own efforts. His life was transformed by that insight, and he began to proclaim this message, which is the essence of the Christian gospel. And with that good news, Luther helped ignite the Protestant Reformation.

So, as I look at the church of Jesus Christ today, I am troubled by the tragedy of churches functioning without faith, as if faith were not important. These churches have great programs, great leadership and management skills, and great marketing programs, but where is the faith? We seem to have lost the key to salvation, the key to the good news of Jesus Christ, the key to healing from guilt and shame and inadequacy.

We seem to have lost our faith.

The Truth About Faith

The longer I live, the more I realize that Christians divide into two camps—those who live victoriously and those who live defeated lives. The apostle John gives us the secret of the victorious Christian life, and the secret is simple: "For everyone who has been born of God overcomes the world. And this is the victory that has overcome the world—our faith" (1 John 5:4). Did you catch the secret in that verse? The secret to victory is absolute trust in God and unswerving obedience to his commands. Faith is the victory.

By faith, we give our lives to God. By faith, we surrender control of our lives to him. We do this not to impress God or to buy his favor but as an expression of gratitude to God for the salvation he freely gives us through Jesus Christ.

We need to remember that there is faith—and there is "faith." Much of what we call faith is not authentic faith at all. It is possible to be very religious, to engage in religious activities, to impress other people with the intensity of our religion—but to be completely devoid of authentic faith. As an anonymous writer once observed, we may offer sacrifices like Cain, weep like Esau, serve like Gehazi, flee Sodom like Lot's wife, minister like Korah the Levite, prophesy like King Saul, make long prayers like the Pharisees, be a disciple like Judas, be a seeker like the rich young ruler, and tremble like Felix— and all without faith. All of these people were deeply religious, but none of them had faith. There is nothing in the world as futile as being religious yet lost, maintaining a form of religion but lacking in faith.

We all need to understand two principles about faith.

First, there is no power whatsoever in our faith. The power comes from the Object of our faith, not from faith itself. If you have faith that you can fly and you launch yourself from the top of a twenty-story building, I guarantee that you will be severely disappointed. But if you have faith in the Lord Jesus Christ and his power, then you will live a victorious Christian life. That kind of faith can move mountains because it is focused on Jesus, the Source of all power.

Second, faith has nothing to do with feelings. Authentic faith in Christ does not rise and fall with our emotions. Faith is a decision to act consistently with God's promises. We can act in faith even when we are down in the dumps emotionally. We may not feel we are bubbling over with faith, yet we can still say, "God said it, I believe it, and that settles it." And often, when we act in accordance with our faith, our feelings will follow.

In Judges 7, we see the budding faith of Gideon. In Judges 6, we saw that when God called Gideon, he was doubtful, distrustful, and insecure. He couldn't bring himself to believe that God would do what he said. But in Judges 7, we see Gideon's faith beginning to bud like a flower in springtime. Soon it will open into full bloom.

Gideon is learning to trust the Lord. He is about to take God fully at his word and act boldly on the belief that God will do what he says he will do:

> Then Jerubbaal (that is, Gideon) and all the people who were with him rose early and encamped beside the spring of Harod. And the camp of Midian was north of them, by the hill of Moreh, in the valley.
>
> The LORD said to Gideon, "The people with you are too many for me to give the Midianites into their hand, lest Israel boast over me, saying, 'My own hand has saved me.' Now therefore proclaim in the ears of the people, saying, 'Whoever is fearful and trembling, let him return home and hurry away from Mount Gilead.'" Then 22,000 of the people returned, and 10,000 remained (7:1-3).

God is about to turn the tables on Gideon. In Judges 6, Gideon kept saying to God, "Show me." And God graciously, patiently proved himself to Gideon again and again. He proved himself through the supernatural flame of the sacrifice and through the two fleeces Gideon laid out. Every time Gideon said, "Show me," God gave him proof.

So Gideon came to trust in the promises of God. But now it's God's turn to say, "Show me." God tells Gideon, in effect, "Now it's your turn to show me. I want you to show me that your faith is real. Do you trust me, Gideon? Then show me."

As the chapter opens, Gideon has gathered his army—32,000 men of Israel—beside the spring of Harod. The Midianite forces are encamped in a valley to the north of them. As we will see in Judges 8, the Midianite forces number 135,000 men. So the odds are already tilted steeply against Israel, and Gideon is undoubtedly worried about their prospects.

Then God tells Gideon he has *too many* soldiers.

Gideon must have been thunderstruck. Though the passage doesn't tell us, I'm sure Gideon must have protested, "Lord, you can't be serious! How can I have too many soldiers? The Midianites outnumber us more than four to one! How can you ask me to downsize my army even further?"

But the Lord has an excellent reason for reducing the size of Gideon's army. "If you defeat the Midianites with an army of 32,000 men," God replies, in effect, "the people of Israel will boast and say, 'We saved ourselves—we don't need God.' So I want you to pare your army down. Tell your soldiers that whoever is afraid may go home."

As it turned out, more than two-thirds of Gideon's soldiers were cowards. As a result, 22,000 soldiers walked away from the battle-field, leaving a force of 10,000 brave Israelites to face the Midianites. This meant that the Israelites were overmatched by a factor of 13.5 to 1. By any rational measure, the Israelites didn't stand a chance.

But the odds were about to get much worse.

Gideon's Three Hundred Men

If Gideon's cause was hopeless with a force of 32,000 men, it was even more hopeless with 10,000. But God was about to tilt the playing field one more time:

And the LORD said to Gideon, "The people are still too many. Take them down to the water, and I will test them for you there, and anyone of whom I say to you, 'This one shall go with you,' shall go with you, and anyone of whom I say to you, 'This one shall not go with you,' shall not go." So he brought the people down to the water. And the LORD said to Gideon, "Every one who laps the water with his tongue, as a dog laps, you shall set by himself. Likewise, every one who kneels down to drink." And the number of those who lapped, putting their hands to their mouths, was 300 men, but all the rest of the people knelt down to drink water. And the LORD said to Gideon, "With the 300 men who lapped I will save you and give the Midianites into your hand, and let all the others go every man to his home." So the people took provisions in their hands, and their trumpets. And he sent all the rest of Israel every man to his tent, but retained the 300 men. And the camp of Midian was below him in the valley (Judges 7:4-8).

We live in a culture that is impressed with numbers, with odds and percentages and statistics. But numbers do not make the victory. Faith is the victory.

In all too many churches today, Christians live by statistics, not faith. We need to learn to live by God's mathematical formula, which states, "One plus God equals a majority." Any worldly military expert will tell you that 135,000 soldiers trumps 32,000 or 10,000 soldiers. And 135,000 soldiers versus 300 soldiers is simply too absurd a ratio to contemplate.

Yet God operates on a different mathematical scale. He says to Gideon, "I can't use all these people. Send most of them home." And

Gideon, whose faith was bolstered by the supernatural fire, the wet fleece, and the dry fleece, now has to begin questioning his own sanity. He has to be asking himself, *Am I hearing God correctly? The Midianites have 135,000 soldiers plus camels.* (This, by the way, is the first recorded use of camels as beasts of war in the history of mankind. This is significant because a foot soldier is no match for an attacker mounted on camelback.) As Gideon considered the enemy he faced, he probably thought, *The Midianites might as well have nuclear weapons!*

But God doesn't care whether the Midianites have 135,000 soldiers plus camels or a billion-man army with nuclear weapons. God wants to bring Gideon to a place in his faith where the disparity between the two human armies means nothing to him. God wants Gideon to understand that, even with all their soldiers and camels, the Midianites are hopelessly outgunned. Why? Because Yahweh, Maker of Heaven and Earth, fights on the side of his people Israel.

Why did God test Gideon's faith in this way? Why does God test our faith in him? Why does he put us in positions where we have to prove our trust in him and in his promise never to leave us nor forsake us? I believe God puts our faith to the test for two reasons.

First, God wants to reveal to us the true nature of our faith. As Christians, we claim to have faith. But is our faith just an intellectual assent to a creed—or a realistic willingness to risk everything on his promises? Is our faith just words—or do we express our faith through obedient action?

Second, God wants to strengthen our faith. Every time our faith is tested and we learn to trust him a little more, our faith grows stronger. The stronger our faith, the more fully he is able to carry out his purpose through our lives. His purpose for us is that we be conformed to the image of Christ (see Romans 8:29)—that we become increasingly more Christlike in our character and obedience.

God tested Gideon in order to reveal the true nature of Gideon's faith and to strengthen his faith. God knew that Gideon was inclined to place his trust in numbers, not in God himself. Did you know that God tests our faith so that he can prove himself to us?

Gideon's 32,000 soldiers were too many. God couldn't use them, so he told Gideon to limit his forces to 300 men. When Gideon went up against the Midianites, he would be facing a 450 to 1 numerical disadvantage. From a human standpoint, God was sending Gideon on a suicide mission. But God loves hopeless odds. He loves an impossible challenge. It has been said that "little is much when God is in it." This was never more true than on the day of Gideon's battle.

In God's economy, numbers are nothing. Faith is everything. Faith in God alone is the victory.

If You Were Gideon

Put yourself in Gideon's sandals. He has tried everything to ascertain and confirm God's will. He has used an offering and laid out fleeces, yet he is still not sure he can trust God's promises. God is saying 32,000 is too many, 10,000 is too many, 300 soldiers is just right.

The God who created the universe could have spoken one word and turned the entire Midianite army to dust. The Midianites were not God's problem. The Midianites were God's chosen instrument. He was using them to chasten his children and teach them a lesson about trusting him. Unbelievers are never a problem for God. But he anguishes over his people and longs for them to love him and trust him. He yearns for his people to place their complete trust in his promises, no matter what.

And God has the same longing for you and me. God can destroy our enemies with a snap of his fingers. But it's much harder for him to overcome the dullness of our hearts. God can answer all our prayers and meet all our needs with a single word, but the problem of our lack of faith is much harder to solve. God has given us free will and he will not violate or trample our freedom. So we must learn to trust him and obey him daily as we experience his love and grace.

Our growth and our character mean far more to God than the obstacles and battles we face. He longs for us to manifest a strong, obedient faith in him. He wants to bring us to a point where we can say, like Job, "Though he slay me, I will hope in him" (Job 13:15). Doubt sees a forest of obstacles, but faith sees a path through the forest.

Human beings are control freaks. We love being in control, and we can't stand giving up control to anyone, even God. Though we know that God is all-knowing, all-wise, and all-loving, we resist surrendering control of our lives to him. But once we willingly yield control to him, we experience the peace of knowing that our loving Creator controls our destiny. There is no greater joy in life than seeing God work out his will through our lives and even through our weakness. As the apostle Paul wrote, "But he said to me, 'My grace is sufficient for you, for my power is made perfect in weakness.' Therefore I will boast all the more gladly of my weaknesses, so that the power of Christ may rest upon me" (2 Corinthians 12:9).

God is at his greatest when we are at our weakest. Remember these words: "If you can explain it, then God did not do it." That's the motto of Leading The Way ministries and The Church of The Apostles. If something happened and you can explain it as a result of my clever strategy, my brilliance, my hard work, and my human strength, *then God didn't do it*. I did it. And God help us all if I did it.

I imagine that Gideon experienced doubts and anxiety as he whittled his army down from 32,000 to 300 in obedience to the word of God. But the important thing is: *Gideon obeyed.* He may have had questions in his mind, *but he obeyed anyway.* He may have wondered how God was going to prevail against overwhelming odds, *but he obeyed anyway.* His emotions were churning, and he had to push thoughts of defeat and slaughter out of his mind, *but he obeyed anyway.* Gideon did not act on emotion. He did not act on his doubts. He acted on his faith. He acted in obedience.

One of the first things God did was to remove all the doubters, the fearful, and the fainthearted from Gideon's ranks and send them home. Fear and doubt are contagious. God made sure that he removed cowards from Gideon's army before their pessimism could go viral. God took only the faithful few into battle. He still works the same way today.

This doesn't mean that the remaining few were without fear. I'm sure that many who remained with Gideon had knocking knees and butterflies in their stomachs. But they managed their emotions through faith. They acted on their trust in God, not their fear of the Midianites. They committed themselves in obedience to God regardless of their emotions. They were right where they wanted to be, following the God of Israel into battle.

Everyone has fear in the face of danger. What divides those who go home from those who fight is a simple choice. Those who went home allowed their fears to govern their actions. Those who stayed with Gideon allowed faith to govern their fears.

God's Formula for Faithful Followers

I have seen it many times over my decades of ministry: A Christian prays to God for some deep need. That person weeps tears of anguish while crying out to God. And God answers that prayer and meets that need.

And once the need is met, the Christian steals the credit that rightfully belongs to God. It's a syndrome I call "pride after victory," and it's a way of robbing God of his glory. God will not have his glory stolen from him, and that is why he told Gideon to whittle down the number of soldiers he would take into battle. As John Wesley once said, "Give me a hundred men who fear nothing but sin and love nothing but God, and I will shake the gates of hell."

There is no more powerful force in this world than a believer or small group of believers who are filled with faith and committed to obedience. There is nothing more unstoppable than a faithful remnant with absolute trust in God's promises. As you search the Scriptures and scour the pages of history, you find that God rarely uses the masses, the majorities, the vast armies. He does his most amazing work through a faithful few.

God preserved the human race through the faithful actions of Noah and his family. Moses sent twelve spies into the land of Canaan—but only two (Joshua and Caleb) brought back a report of faith and confidence in God; the majority brought back a report of faithlessness and pessimism. During Israel's exile, God used two faithful Jewish people, Esther and Mordecai, to save the Jewish race from genocide. And in the New Testament, Jesus called the Twelve (with the exception of Judas) to form the nucleus of his new community, the church.

God always uses small numbers of people who are intensely committed to him. Not the masses, not the vast armies—the faithful few.

Gideon's victory lay in his obedience to God's strategy. Gideon did not operate from a human strategy, but a divine strategy. That was the secret to victory. Gideon didn't trust in the arm of man or the sword of iron. He trusted in the promises of God. The Israelite army had no special military equipment, no special weaponry, no great military traditions, no brilliant generals. They didn't even have any camels. They had nothing but an insecure but obedient leader named Gideon—and an almighty God.

"For the LORD and for Gideon!"

After God had whittled down Gideon's army from 32,000 to 300, God sent Gideon on a secret mission:

> That same night the LORD said to him, "Arise, go down against the camp, for I have given it into your hand. But if you are afraid to go down, go down to the camp with Purah your servant. And you shall hear what they say, and afterward your hands shall be strengthened to go down against the camp." Then he went down with Purah his servant to the outposts of the armed men who were in the camp. And the Midianites and the Amale-kites and all the people of the East lay along the valley like locusts in abundance, and their camels were without number, as the sand that is on the seashore in abundance. When Gideon came, behold, a man was telling a dream to his comrade. And he said, "Behold, I dreamed a dream, and behold, a cake of barley bread tumbled into the camp of Midian and came to the tent and struck it so that it fell and turned it upside down, so that the tent lay flat." And his comrade answered, "This is no other than the sword of Gideon the son of Joash, a man of Israel; God has given into his hand Midian and all the camp."
>
> As soon as Gideon heard the telling of the dream and its interpretation, he worshiped. And he returned to the camp of Israel and said, "Arise, for the LORD has given the host of Midian into your hand." And he divided the

300 men into three companies and put trumpets into the hands of all of them and empty jars, with torches inside the jars. And he said to them, "Look at me, and do likewise. When I come to the outskirts of the camp, do as I do. When I blow the trumpet, I and all who are with me, then blow the trumpets also on every side of all the camp and shout, 'For the Lord and for Gideon'" (Judges 7:9-18).

God has already assured Gideon three times, but he obviously knew that Gideon needed even further encouragement before the battle. So God sent Gideon and his servant on a secret spy mission to the outposts of the Midianite camp. At first, the sight of all the enemy warriors and their camels probably did little to encourage Gideon.

But as Gideon and his servant eavesdropped on the enemy sentries, they heard one of them describing a dream—and it was a dream of defeat for the Midianite forces. Though the Midianites outnumbered the Israelites by a factor of 450 to 1, the Midianite soldier believed his people were doomed. The symbol of the cake of barley bread is significant. Barley bread was the food of the poor. God was saying to Gideon through the dream of the Midianite, "I am going to give the victory to you, to the poorest of the poor."

Gideon understood the symbolism. The moment he heard the Midianite describe his dream, Gideon went straight to his knees and worshiped the Lord—practically in the enemy camp! Gideon undoubtedly remembered how patient God had been with him and how God had kept promise after promise to Israel. So Gideon praised God. Then he returned to the camp of Israel and summoned his 300 men, divided them into three companies, and armed them with strange weaponry: trumpets, empty jars, and torches. He gave his men a battle cry: "For the LORD and for Gideon."

Israelites would have to fight the battle, but they would fight in the knowledge that the battle was already won.

This account reminds me of the spiritual warfare you and I face every day. We have to fight this battle—but like Gideon's army, we fight in the knowledge that the battle has already been won. Jesus has won the battle on the cross.

The apostle Paul wrote, "For we do not wrestle against flesh and blood, but against the rulers, against the authorities, against the cosmic powers over this present darkness, against the spiritual forces of evil in the heavenly places" (Ephesians 6:12). We may face an enemy of ten million warriors—but we don't need an army of equal size to even the odds. People are not our enemy. In fact, our enemy is not flesh and blood. We fight a spiritual battle with spiritual weapons. We fight against spiritual forces of evil, but God, the Creator of the universe, is on our side, and our enemy doesn't stand a chance. You and I have but to secure our victory by obeying our victorious general, the Lord Jesus Christ.

It's significant that Gideon took time near the enemy camp to worship the Lord. Many Christians have a hard time worshiping. If worship is a struggle for you, perhaps the reason is that something inside you refuses to bow to the will of God. Worship is the outward expression of an inward submission to God. We cannot authentically worship on the outside if we are rebellious on the inside.

We are like the child in the classroom who refused to obey his teacher. The teacher said, again and again, "Sit down!" After the child had repeatedly refused to obey, the teacher went to him, placed her hands on his shoulders, and physically pushed him into his seat.

The child scowled and said, "I may be sitting down on the outside, but I'm standing up on the inside."

Many of us go through the motions of worship on the outside, but inside we are standing up and rebelling against God. That's why we struggle in worship. We cannot truly worship the Lord until we have surrendered to him. If you cannot bow the knee and worship the living God, your will is not submitted to his will. Without faith, it is impossible to please God. Faith is the victory.

Gideon's secret mission to the camp of the Midianites renewed and strengthened his faith. God gave Gideon wisdom to prepare his army for the battle and courage to lead his army. But it would not be a strong arm and the keen sword of the Israelites that would win the battle.

The battle is the Lord's. God had already struck terror into the hearts of the Midianites. The defeat of Israel's enemy was a foregone conclusion.

The Defeat of Midian

The concluding verses of Judges 7 reveal the outcome of the battle. It is undoubtedly one of the strangest and most unlikely incidents in military history:

> So Gideon and the hundred men who were with him came to the outskirts of the camp at the beginning of the middle watch, when they had just set the watch. And they blew the trumpets and smashed the jars that were in their hands. Then the three companies blew the trumpets and broke the jars. They held in their left hands the torches, and in their right hands the trumpets to blow. And they cried out, "A sword for the LORD and for Gideon!" Every man stood in his place around the camp,

and all the army ran. They cried out and fled. When they blew the 300 trumpets, the LORD set every man's sword against his comrade and against all the army. And the army fled as far as Beth-shittah toward Zererah, as far as the border of Abel-meholah, by Tabbath. And the men of Israel were called out from Naphtali and from Asher and from all Manasseh, and they pursued after Midian.

Gideon sent messengers throughout all the hill country of Ephraim, saying, "Come down against the Midianites and capture the waters against them, as far as Beth-barah, and also the Jordan." So all the men of Ephraim were called out, and they captured the waters as far as Beth-barah, and also the Jordan. And they captured the two princes of Midian, Oreb and Zeeb. They killed Oreb at the rock of Oreb, and Zeeb they killed at the winepress of Zeeb. Then they pursued Midian, and they brought the heads of Oreb and Zeeb to Gideon across the Jordan (7:19-25).

This vast army of 135,000 heavily armed warriors was so panic-stricken by the sound of the trumpets that they turned their swords on each other. Those who survived the fratricide fled in panic and terror from 300 Israelites and their trumpets. Imagine several divisions of United States Marines fleeing from a high-school marching band—that's how ludicrous this scene truly is. But of course, it wasn't the trumpets that won the battle. God, who struck fear into the hearts of Israel's enemies, won the battle.

On Easter Sunday 1799, the army of Napoleon Bonaparte surrounded the Austrian village of Feldkirch. The villagers were terrified. They had no way of defending themselves against the ruthless conqueror from France. They were ready to raise the white flag of surrender.

But the bishop of the church urged them not to surrender just yet. "This is Easter Sunday," he said. "This is the day we celebrate the resurrection of our King, Jesus the Lord. Before we surrender our village, let us have one moment of triumph. Let us ring all the bells of the town in celebration of our Lord's triumph over death."

The people of the town agreed. Soon the church bells pealed out the sound of celebration. The joyful noise of victory filled the air.

Outside the village, Napoleon's army was filled with consternation. What did the ringing of the bells mean? Napoleon's generals conferred, and they concluded that there could be only one explanation: the Austrian army must have arrived during the night to defend the town.

The bells of the church were still ringing as the army of Napoleon turned away and retreated.

The spiritual battles you face have already been won. The victory is yours. Your enemy cannot stand against you because Jesus has won the battle on the cross of Calvary.

There will be times when you wonder, *Where is my victory? Where is the answer to my prayer?* At such times, remind yourself that faith is the victory, and the victory has been won. Don't put your trust in people or money or possessions or your own strength and ingenuity. Place your confidence solely in the Lord.

Let the budding faith of Gideon be an example to you. Faith is the victory that overcomes the world.

6

The Snare of
Prosperity

The Scottish essayist Thomas Carlyle observed, "Adversity is
sometimes hard upon a man; but for one man who can stand
prosperity there are a hundred that will stand adversity."[31] I
have observed this to be true. Many people successfully maintain
their faith and moral virtue under the pressure of adversity—then
completely fail the test of success. One Old Testament hero who
tragically flunked the success test was Gideon.

It seems doubly sad when a man who passes so many other tests
in life fails the final test, the success test. It is heartbreaking to see a
man start out well, and then finish badly. The Gideon we encounter near the end of Judges 8 has undergone a change from the insecure, reluctant hero we first meet in Judges 6. The contrast is stark
and tragic. Gideon starts out in humility but ends in pride. He starts
out seeking God's glory but ends up ambitious for his own glory.

While Gideon did many things right following his success in the battle against the Midianites, he failed the ultimate test. His failure led to the moral and spiritual backsliding of the entire nation of Israel.

The story of Gideon in Judges 8 continues following the miraculous defeat of the Midianites. Now Gideon proceeds to mop up after the victory, pursuing the defeated Midianite leaders as they flee:

> Then the men of Ephraim said to him, "What is this that you have done to us, not to call us when you went to fight against Midian?" And they accused him fiercely. And he said to them, "What have I done now in comparison with you? Is not the gleaning of the grapes of Ephraim better than the grape harvest of Abiezer? God has given into your hands the princes of Midian, Oreb and Zeeb. What have I been able to do in comparison with you?" Then their anger against him subsided when he said this.
>
> And Gideon came to the Jordan and crossed over, he and the 300 men who were with him, exhausted yet pursuing. So he said to the men of Succoth, "Please give loaves of bread to the people who follow me, for they are exhausted, and I am pursuing after Zebah and Zalmunna, the kings of Midian." And the officials of Succoth said, "Are the hands of Zebah and Zalmunna already in your hand, that we should give bread to your army?" So Gideon said, "Well then, when the LORD has given Zebah and Zalmunna into my hand, I will flail your flesh with the thorns of the wilderness and with briers." And from there he went up to Penuel, and spoke to them in the same way, and the men of Penuel answered him as the men of Succoth had answered. And he said

to the men of Penuel, "When I come again in peace, I will break down this tower."

Now Zebah and Zalmunna were in Karkor with their army, about 15,000 men, all who were left of all the army of the people of the East, for there had fallen 120,000 men who drew the sword. And Gideon went up by the way of the tent dwellers east of Nobah and Jogbehah and attacked the army, for the army felt secure. And Zebah and Zalmunna fled, and he pursued them and captured the two kings of Midian, Zebah and Zalmunna, and he threw all the army into a panic.

Then Gideon the son of Joash returned from the battle by the ascent of Heres. And he captured a young man of Succoth and questioned him. And he wrote down for him the officials and elders of Succoth, seventy-seven men. And he came to the men of Succoth and said, "Behold Zebah and Zalmunna, about whom you taunted me, saying, 'Are the hands of Zebah and Zalmunna already in your hand, that we should give bread to your men who are exhausted?'" And he took the elders of the city, and he took thorns of the wilderness and briers and with them taught the men of Succoth a lesson. And he broke down the tower of Penuel and killed the men of the city.

Then he said to Zebah and Zalmunna, "Where are the men whom you killed at Tabor?" They answered, "As you are, so were they. Every one of them resembled the son of a king." And he said, "They were my brothers, the sons of my mother. As the LORD lives, if you had saved them alive, I would not kill you." So he said to Jether his firstborn, "Rise and kill them!" But the young man did not draw his sword, for he was afraid, because he was still a young man. Then Zebah and Zalmunna said, "Rise yourself and fall upon us, for as the man is, so is his strength." And Gideon arose and killed Zebah and Zalmunna, and he took the crescent ornaments that were on the necks of their camels (Judges 8:1-21).

At the end of Judges 7, following the defeat of the Midianites, Gideon sent messengers into the region of Israel controlled by the tribe of Ephraim. His message to the Ephraimites was to chase down two of the fleeing Midianite leaders, Oreb and Zeeb. The Ephraimites pursued and killed Oreb and Zeeb and sent their heads to Gideon as proof that they had accomplished their mission.

Yet the men of Ephraim were critical of Gideon, who was of the tribe of Manasseh. In the book of Genesis, Ephraim and Manasseh were brothers, the sons of Joseph (see Genesis 46:20). So the tribes of Ephraim and Manasseh were actually half-tribes comprising the tribe of Joseph. Ephraim and Manasseh became part of the tribes of Israel by the sovereign choice of God. So the Ephraimites were closely related to Gideon, and were, in an extended-family sense, Gideon's brothers. As often happens in families, there was sibling rivalry between these brothers.

Bruised Egos

Gideon had given the Ephraimites a major role in the mop-up after the battle so that they would share in the credit and glory. Yet they were angry with Gideon for not including them in the main attack on the Midianite camp. They wanted the credit for the defeat of Midian, and their feelings were hurt and they were angry because they were not part of the select three hundred.

The Ephraimites didn't understand that it was God, not Gideon, who had chosen the three hundred. It was God's plan from beginning to end. God conceived, confirmed, and executed the plan. It was a divine strategy, not Gideon's strategy. The Ephraimites said, in effect, "You must take our opinion into account. What were you thinking, calling us in only after the battle was already won? Why weren't we consulted first? Why did you bring us in only for the mop-up operation?"

The Ephraimites are displaying a common human failing—a critical spirit. When people have a critical spirit, they usually mask the real reason for their criticism. They know they would look foolish if they said, "You really bruised my ego. You really offended my pompous pride." That's really what it's all about, but no one wants to admit it. So they mask their bruised egos with spiritual-sounding rationales and moralistic language. They often attribute their criticism to vague, unnamed sources: "People are saying…" or "There's talk going around…"

You may remember the story of Miriam and Aaron, the brother and sister of Moses (see Numbers 12). They became angry with Moses because he had married a dark-skinned Cushite woman. Perhaps not wanting to admit that they were motivated by racism, they attacked the leadership role of Moses. They didn't like his leadership style, the attention and fame he received, and the fact that Moses got the limelight and they didn't. Aaron, of course, was the high priest and Miriam was the music leader of Israel, but they wanted to be on the same level as Moses himself. So Miriam and Aaron complained, "Has the LORD indeed spoken only through Moses? Has he not spoken through us also?" (Numbers 12:1-2).

But the real reason for their critical attitude toward Moses was his dark-skinned wife. M.R. DeHaan, founder of the Radio Bible Class, once said, "It is a dead giveaway when you meet a person who is always criticizing and finding fault with another. Ninety-nine times out of a hundred, he's trying to divert attention from his own sins by pointing an accusing finger at someone else." And Reformed clergyman Thomas De Witt Talmage (1832–1902) observed, "Without exception, the people who have the greatest number of faults are themselves the most merciless in their criticism of others. They spend their lives looking for something lowly rather than something lofty." [32]

People also are critical of others out of a sense of self-righteousness and moral superiority. By condemning and criticizing you, I make myself out to be morally superior to you. This is the essence of Pharisaism—making oneself appear more holy by condemning the supposed sins of others.

Nowadays, it's fashionable to condemn so-called "Victorian morality," but I believe that the moral values of the Victorian era—which were greatly influenced by the life and values of Queen Victoria herself—had a positive influence on our culture. Queen Victoria was one of the most godly, Christ-centered monarchs the modern world has known.

Like most British monarchs, Queen Victoria spent the summer months in Balmoral Castle in Scotland. One warm Sunday afternoon, the queen boarded a boat and had her attendants row her around on the lake behind the castle. Of course, wherever the queen went, she attracted a crowd, so people were watching from the shore as she was out on the lake.

One self-righteous woman in the crowd was indignant. She turned to a clergyman standing nearby and said, "Look at that! It's disgusting that the queen would have her staff doing work on the Lord's Day!"

The clergyman replied, "Well, ma'am, do you remember that

Jesus went out on the Sea of Galilee in a boat, and he had the disciples row him around on the Sabbath?"

"Well," the woman replied, "two wrongs don't make a right!"

You have undoubtedly met people like her. I certainly have. Unfortunately, all too many Christians believe they have received "the spiritual gift of criticism," and they practice it at every opportunity.

Sometimes, we as parents come across as overly critical, particularly in dealing with our teenagers. Psychologist Larry Kubiak says that the average parent spends only fourteen minutes per day communicating with his or her teenage children. Twelve of those minutes typically involve negative communication (scolding, nagging, and so forth), one minute is neutral, and one minute is positive or affirming.[33]

It's crucial when dealing with teenagers to avoid belittling their character. That means no name-calling, no sarcasm, no yelling. We should avoid forcing kids into endeavors where they have no aptitude and would end up feeling embarrassed. We need to listen to teens and praise them when praise is due. If they lose control and begin yelling or name-calling, it's all the more important that we maintain control, stay calm, and lower our voices.

Some parents praise their children all the time for everything, and such praise quickly becomes empty and meaningless. The most effective praise affirms not just accomplishments but evidence of faith, character growth, integrity, and initiative. What you praise, you'll get more of. If you want to see young people demonstrating Christlike character and boldly witnessing to their friends, if you want them to show kindness to others while standing firm against peer pressure, then praise that behavior. Instead of always catching them doing wrong, catch them in the act of doing right—and affirm them for it.

The Criticism Test

It's instructive to note how Gideon responded when he was criticized by his brothers. They treated him harshly, and Gideon did not become defensive. He responded with grace and wisdom. He seemed to intuitively understand the principle of Proverbs 15:1,

> A soft answer turns away wrath,
> > but a harsh word stirs up anger.

and Proverbs 16:32,

> Whoever is slow to anger is better than the mighty,
> > and he who rules his spirit than he who takes a city.

Gideon could have responded with bitter words of his own, but instead, he swallowed his pride and praised the Ephraimites who criticized him. "What have I done now in comparison with you?" he said. "Is not the gleaning of the grapes of Ephraim better than the grape harvest of Abiezer? God has given into your hands the princes of Midian, Oreb and Zeeb. What have I been able to do in comparison with you?" (Judges 8:1-2).

The metaphor of the grape harvest was Gideon's way of saying, "My poor accomplishments aren't worthy to be compared with what you have done. My entire grape harvest doesn't even measure up to the grapes that are left behind for the gleaners in your vineyards." Gideon humbled himself in order to defuse the situation and make peace with his brothers. Gideon had passed the criticism test. He responded to unfair criticism with grace, wisdom, and godly character.

By contrast, Gideon dealt harshly with those who were guilty of treason. After leaving the Ephraimites, Gideon and his three hundred men crossed the Jordan and continued to pursue the two remaining Midianite kings, Zebah and Zalmunna. At two towns, Succoth and Peniel, Gideon stopped and asked for provisions so that he could continue the pursuit. But the men in those towns refused to help, and they taunted Gideon instead. So Gideon continued on his way without their aid and captured the two Midianite kings.

When Gideon returned to Succoth, he took the elders of the city who had taunted him and flogged them with thorny briers because they had acted treasonously toward Gideon when he was ridding the nation of the foreign oppressors. Gideon also went to Peniel, where he and his men destroyed the tower, killing the men who had taken refuge inside.

It may seem harsh for Gideon to punish the men of Succoth and Peniel so severely, especially after showing grace to the Ephraimites. But there's no comparison between the wounded egos of the Ephraimites and the outright treason and rebellion of Succoth and Peniel. The men of Succoth and Peniel hindered God's chosen leader as he pursued the enemies of Israel. They committed a grievous crime against Yahweh and against the nation of Israel by actually giving aid to Israel's oppressive enemies, the Midianites. In order for Gideon to deliver Israel, the traitors had to be exposed and punished. Gideon's harsh actions in those cities were justified.

The Popularity Test

The next test Gideon faced was the personal popularity test. Following his victory over the Midianites, the people of Israel wanted to make him their king:

> Then the men of Israel said to Gideon, "Rule over us, you and your son and your grandson also, for you have saved us from the hand of Midian." Gideon said to them,

"I will not rule over you, and my son will not rule over
you; the LORD will rule over you" (Judges 8:22-23).

The Israelites were ready to set up a hereditary monarchy, with
Gideon and his descendants ruling over them. In their eyes, Gideon
had proved himself worthy. The people wanted a king, and Gideon's
success seemed to qualify him for the position.

It was a test of Gideon's character. Could he resist the temptation
to parlay his popularity and his military victory (which was really
the Lord's victory, not Gideon's) into political power? Gideon passed
that test with flying colors. He resisted the temptation and said, "I
will not rule over you... The LORD will rule over you."

Gideon knew his people were on the verge of committing a sin
that had brought the nation down in failure and defeat again and
again. Gideon rightly understood that the Achilles' heel of the Israelite people was their tendency, whenever God delivered them, to
give credit to some human hero. The Israelites repeatedly forgot that
God delivered them, not some man. Gideon knew that God, not
Gideon, struck fear in the hearts of the Midianites, so he refused to
steal the glory that belonged to God alone.

Gideon knew that God was the savior of Israel. God was the king
of Israel. God was the provider and ruler of Israel, and the source of
all of Israel's blessings. Even Gideon's calling to lead Israel came from
the Holy Spirit. Gideon had not sought a leadership role and didn't
feel qualified for leadership. He had simply listened and obeyed.
God had done the rest.

Whenever we put a human being in God's place, disaster follows.
Every Israelite understood the reason that God, in his design of the
tabernacle, placed the mercy seat in the Holy of Holies, the inner-
most sanctuary of the tabernacle. It was there as a visual reminder

that God was on his throne, ruling over his people. Every Israelite understood that Yahweh was their king, and the mercy seat represented his throne.

Gideon knew that to set up a rival throne, a human monarchy, would result in the dethronement of Yahweh. It was bad enough that Israel had marginalized God and pushed him to the periphery of their culture. But to dethrone God altogether would have meant the end of the Jewish nation.

So Gideon rejected the people's effort to make him king. And if the narrative had ended at that point, it would have been a happy ending. Gideon had passed the criticism test and the popularity test. Tragically, however, he was about to fail the idolatry test.

The Idolatry Test

It's difficult to understand how Gideon, after proving himself faithful and obedient to God, could have failed the idolatry test so miserably and completely:

> And Gideon said to them, "Let me make a request of you: every one of you give me the earrings from his spoil." (For they had golden earrings, because they were Ishmaelites.) And they answered, "We will willingly give them." And they spread a cloak, and every man threw in it the earrings of his spoil. And the weight of the golden earrings that he requested was 1,700 shekels of gold, besides the crescent ornaments and the pendants and the purple garments worn by the kings of Midian, and besides the collars that were around the necks of their camels. And Gideon made an ephod of it and put it in his city, in Ophrah. And all Israel whored after it there, and it became a snare to Gideon and to his family. So Midian

was subdued before the people of Israel, and they raised
their heads no more. And the land had rest forty years
in the days of Gideon (Judges 8:24-28).

The land had rest, but not Gideon. After he made the golden
ephod, it became a snare, an obstacle, a source of continual hurts
and misery for Gideon and his family. And it was a source of stumbling for the nation of Israel.

You may be asking, what is an ephod and how could it become
an idol? The ephod was a garment, shaped much like an apron,
probably woven from linen thread and embroidered with gold
thread, with a golden breastplate and other adornments. The use of
ephods is described elsewhere in Scripture, for example, in Exodus
28:6-14 and 1 Chronicles 15:27. It was a garment to be worn only
by the high priest. The names of the tribes of Israel were written on
it, and two symbolic precious stones were part of its design. Those
two stones were called the Urim and Thummim, and the stones
were used to discern the will and plan of God. The high priest of
Israel was to wear the ephod once a year while serving at the tabernacle at Shiloh. It was a symbol of God's presence and his rule over
the people of Israel.

Gideon's error was that he wanted to control God's revelation.
He wanted to have direct guidance from God so that he could direct
the people. He had rejected the monarchy and the position of king,
yet he couldn't resist holding on to a measure of power that rightfully belonged to God's high priest. This is a danger—a "snare," as
the book of Judges calls it—that still afflicts the church today.

When you see a church in turmoil, you will likely find that the
conflict is triggered by people who do not recognize God's anointing of church leaders. You will often find conflict surrounding certain individuals who want to have control and preeminence in

the church. They are greedy for power, position, and recognition, and they try to run the church according to secular methodologies. That's why they never receive God's anointing for church leadership, though that doesn't stop them from trying to get their way in the church. The apostle John described one such person in the first-century church: "I have written something to the church, but Diotrephes, who likes to put himself first, does not acknowledge our authority" (3 John 9).

I believe Gideon had good intentions. I can understand how he succumbed to the temptation of wanting to control God's revelation. He figured, *God spoke to me before, and that worked out well. The high priest is off in Shiloh, and I can really do a better job than he can, so I'll take on the role of high priest. I'll wear the ephod and carry out the priestly function here in my home city of Ophrah. If I'm going to be the substitute high priest, then I'll need an ephod of my own.*

Gideon's error was that he began to think that God could not lead Israel without him. So he told the people, "You have gotten all the spoils from the battle, so each of you should contribute one golden ring." Gideon collected the gold and made a beautiful golden ephod. The result of Gideon's error was a national tragedy: "Gideon made an ephod of it and put it in his city, in Ophrah. And all Israel whored after it there, and it became a snare to Gideon and to his family" (8:27).

This is the saddest statement in the entire narrative of Gideon. When the text tells us that Israel "whored after" the golden ephod, it means that Israel became unfaithful to God and worshiped the ephod as an idol. They treated the ephod as an oracle, a magical pipeline to God.

Many people commit the same error today.

In almost every church, you'll find at least a few people who will tell you what God wants you to do. They'll come to you and say, "I have a word from the Lord for you." When I hear that, I scratch my head and say, "That's odd. I spent two hours with the Lord in prayer this morning, and he never mentioned a word of what you just told me. Why did he say this to you and say nothing to me?"

I find that when people come to me with "a word from the Lord," it is usually a message that aligns with something *they* want me to do. Like Gideon, they may sincerely think that God speaks to them, but in reality, they have a fleshly desire for control—so they invoke God and claim his supernatural seal of approval on their personal agenda. And if you say, "I don't believe that's what God wants us to do," they will respond, "Why are you resisting the Lord?"

Poor Gideon. He started out right, but he turned out wrong. His own success ensnared him, and he began to believe his own press clippings. His success gave him an oversized ego, and he believed he could usurp the function of the high priest. As someone once observed, EGO stands for Edging God Out. Gideon deceived himself into thinking that by making a golden ephod, he could serve the Lord. But the ephod he made became an idol, an object of false worship. By making this ephod, Gideon served his own ego and he tragically edged God out.

Over the years, I have seen a number of young people who became attracted to the trappings of ministry, and they became ambitious for a career in ministry. Once they actually got into ministry and discovered the challenges, the temptations, and the pressures, they opted out. According to almost two decades of research conducted by the Francis A. Schaeffer Institute of Church Leadership Development and the Fuller Institute, 60 to 80 percent of those who enter the ministry will have left the ministry within a decade. And at any given time, fully 50 percent of pastors would leave the ministry if they could, but they believe they have no other way of making a living.[34]

Many people have a noble desire to serve God in full-time ministry, but they have failed to discern God's anointing for their lives. You should stay in your area of anointing. The Bible warns against being too ambitious to be a teacher in the church: "Not many of you should become teachers, my brothers, for you know that we who teach will be judged with greater strictness" (James 3:1). If God has not called you to full-time ministry, if that is not your area of anointing, then you should stay out of full-time ministry.

I've seen this same principle in the lives of Christian businessmen. God gives certain people an anointing (or a favor) for business, for working in real estate or banking or technology or some other field of commerce. After a while, however, they branch out into some other area and try to take on too much. They try to work outside their area of anointing and they lose their shirts. They end up discouraged and defeated. Often, they feel that God has misled them, when in reality, they have misled themselves. Stay in the area of your anointing or calling. That's where you'll find God's blessing for your life.

A number of years ago, I had a conversation with a man who left the pastoral ministry, and I asked him why he had left. He replied, "I realized after a few years that sheep do bite. And I couldn't take it."

While I agree that sheep bite, and they sometimes bite the shepherd, that is not the reason this man left the ministry. What he did not know is that when God gives you the anointing for full-time ministry, he gives you the grace to endure the challenges, opposition, and temptations of that calling. When God gives you the anointing of a shepherd of God's flock, he gives you the grace to withstand the bite marks of the sheep.

If God calls you to a new ministry, a new anointing, he will tell you so in a clear way. But don't try to become something you're not. And above all, don't try to take someone else's anointing into your life.

Do you remember the story of David and Goliath in 1 Samuel 17? As David prepared to go out on the field of battle and face Goliath, King Saul put his own armor on David—a helmet of bronze, a coat of mail, and a heavy sword. But Saul's armor was too big for the young shepherd boy. Encumbered by its weight, David couldn't even walk, much less wield a sword. "I cannot go with these," David said as he took the armor off. Then he went out and won the battle armed with nothing but a shepherd's sling and five smooth stones. David had the spiritual wisdom, even at that young age, to stay within his own anointing. By doing so, David made sure that God received the credit and the glory for the victory over Goliath.

Don't go to war in someone else's armor. If you are a doctor, an engineer, an educator, an accountant, a CEO, an entertainer, a sanitation engineer, or a homemaker, stay in your area of anointing. Carry out the ministry God has appointed for you. Serve him faithfully and be his witness, his ambassador, in that area of anointing.

Gideon's Tragic Epitaph

Earlier in this book, when we examined the life of Deborah the judge and prophetess, I observed that Deborah is one of the most remarkable women in the Bible. One of the reasons she is such a great role model is that she resisted the temptation of taking Barak's anointing. She stayed in the area of her anointing and was careful not to usurp Barak's role. It was hard for her to do that because Barak would not step up and lead. He kept trying to abdicate his anointing and surrender his responsibility to Deborah. But to her credit, she remained true to her anointing, and she persevered in prodding Barak to live up to his anointing.

If only Gideon had been as wise as Deborah. Unfortunately, Gideon had a private agenda. He did not want the power of the king or a military ruler—but he craved the role of the high priest. He was ambitious to take on an anointing that did not belong to him. That was his downfall, and the entire nation of Israel suffered as a result.

God had told Israel that the high priest must come from the Levites—not Manasseh, not Ephraim, but the tribe of Levi. But Gideon's ambition was for the priesthood. Beware of ambition, including religious ambition. Beware of coveting a role that is not yours and that is outside your area of anointing.

It is instructive to contrast Abraham, following his military victory in Genesis 14, with Gideon. After Abraham's defeat of King Chedorlaomer and the Elamite forces, Abraham refused to take any of the spoils of victory. But Gideon took the spoils. After his victory, Abraham refused to accept gifts from the king of Sodom, saying, in effect, "I don't want anyone to say that you made me rich; it is God Most High who makes me rich." Abraham gave a tenth of his net worth to Melchizedek, the priestly king of Salem and an Old Testament symbol of Christ. Gideon did not give a tenth to God.

Everything Abraham did and said was designed to give all credit and glory to God. Gideon sought glory for himself by making the ephod for himself—and that is why he ended badly after starting out well. If you want to finish well in the Christian life, if you want to be a blessing to the next generation, then live your life in obedience to the Lord. Stay within your area of anointing. Don't become ambitious for your own glory.

The book of Judges reminds us again and again of our responsibility to influence the next generation, to model godliness and righteousness, to equip the next generation for battle, and to pray daily for our children and grandchildren. The failure of one generation spells disaster for the next.

The story of Gideon ends on this tragic note:

> Jerubbaal [Gideon] the son of Joash went and lived in his own house. Now Gideon had seventy sons, his own offspring, for he had many wives. And his concubine who was in Shechem also bore him a son, and he called his name Abimelech. And Gideon the son of Joash died in a good old age and was buried in the tomb of Joash his father, at Ophrah of the Abiezrites.
>
> As soon as Gideon died, the people of Israel turned again and whored after the Baals and made Baal-berith their god. And the people of Israel did not remember the LORD their God, who had delivered them from the hand of all their enemies on every side, and they did not show steadfast love to the family of Jerubbaal (that is, Gideon) in return for all the good that he had done to Israel (Judges 8:29-35).

For most of his life, Gideon served as a role model of faith and obedience. He listened to God, he followed God's battle plan, and he delivered Israel from the oppression of the Midianites. But he coveted religious glory, and that was his downfall.

Learn from the tragic example of Gideon the judge. He ran his race well, but he stumbled short of the finish line. That is Gideon's tragic epitaph. Don't let it be yours. Run your race and finish strong.

7

Out of the
Ashes of Failure

Over the years, I've met many Christians who were convinced that God couldn't use them because of a shameful sin in their past. They had repented of their sin and were living godly lives—yet their past continued to haunt them and make them feel useless to God. It didn't matter if it was a sin they committed before their conversion to Christ or a major stumble in their Christian walk, their past failure continued to cripple their present-day relationship with God.

Whenever I encounter such people, my message to them is, "I'm glad you understand that sin is a serious matter—but so is the grace of God. You need to come to a place where you can say, *Lord, I have sinned greatly, but I know your grace is greater than my worst sins. You have forgiven me, and you want me to forgive myself.*"

If you are immobilized, feeling God can't use you because of your past sins, I want you to know that this is *not* how God views you. If you see yourself as damaged goods, and you believe God can never use you again, then you have believed a lie—and it's time for you to hear the truth. God does not want you to be immobilized, but there is someone who *does* want you immobilized: the father of lies, Satan himself. Stop listening to his lies. Start believing the truth about God. If you have confessed your sins and repented of them, God has forgiven you. Now it's time to forgive yourself.

Years ago, I counseled a woman who had undergone an abortion many years earlier. As we talked, I walked her through the four steps of restoration from sin: confession, consequences, cleansing, and consecration. She had genuinely and sincerely taken each step. She had confessed her sin with bitter tears. She had suffered the consequences and paid a tremendous personal price. She had experienced God's cleansing forgiveness. And she had consecrated her life to the Lord. Yet she still said, "God cannot use me."

I told her, "That's where you're mistaken. God can use you in a unique way. Your past uniquely qualifies you for a special ministry in God's kingdom. You can minister to other women who are contemplating the choice you made. You can speak with the authority of personal experience. You may save other women from going down the same path—and you may save many lives. Don't let your suffering go to waste. Use it to serve God and serve others. As the psalmist said, 'The sacrifices of God are a broken spirit; a broken and contrite heart, O God, you will not despise'" (Psalm 51:17).

The scars of sin run deep, and some of the hurt may last a lifetime. But God loves a repentant sinner. He forgives us, receives us, and restores us to usefulness in his kingdom. God receives those who are humble and contrite, but he detests the arrogant and self-righteous. He opposes the proud, the ones who are unwilling to humble themselves and confess their sins. He resists those who rationalize their sins.

The playwright Oscar Wilde had a legendary reputation for arrogance. One night, he arrived at a dinner party after a dismal opening night performance of one of his plays. When the other guests asked how his play was received, he reportedly said, "The play was a great success. The audience was a total failure."

God resists the prideful and restores the humble, and he is eager to use those who are brokenhearted over their sins. He takes our unique experiences, including our shame and regret, and weaves them into blessing for others and glory for himself. We serve a God who longs to give us beauty in place of ashes, the oil of gladness in place of mourning, and a garment of praise instead of a faint spirit (see Isaiah 61:3). And one of the greatest examples of this principle is Samson.

Floating with the Current

The story of Samson is widely known—and widely misunderstood. Though the account is familiar, it has been distorted in the public consciousness by Hollywood movies and inaccurate retellings. An image of Samson has been created that is false and unbiblical. Both Christians and non-Christians have a false perception of Samson.

The most common image of Samson is that of a comic book superhero. He is a man of superpowers and super-strength, with a perfectly chiseled body like that of Arnold Schwarzenegger in his prime. But that is not the authentic, historical Samson depicted in Judges 14.

Samson's strength did not come from pumping iron or from taking steroids. His strength was not perfected on a StairMaster or a weight machine. His strength was not natural; it was supernatural. His strength was a gift of God, poured into him by the Holy Spirit to be used in service to God.

Eventually, sin robbed him of his strength—yet God in his grace overruled Samson's sin. Yes, Samson still had to pay the consequences of his sin, but his failure did not end his usefulness to God. After Samson repented, God used that repentance to achieve his purpose.

For many years, I avoided preaching and teaching from the life of Samson. Only recently did it become clear to me why I shied away from this man's life: the story of Samson depresses me. He represents squandered opportunities and the misuse of God's gifts. He's an example of what happens to a man who is incredibly gifted but undisciplined and who will not channel his gifts in obedience to God's commands.

Samson was strong in his battles against man and animals, but he was weak in his dealings with pagan women. God called Samson to declare war on the enemies of Israel, but Samson wouldn't stop fraternizing with enemy women. Any soldier who fraternizes with the enemy betrays himself and the cause he serves.

As the apostle James warns, "You adulterous people! Do you not know that friendship with the world is enmity with God? Therefore whoever wishes to be a friend of the world makes himself an enemy of God" (James 4:4). Samson fought the battles of the Lord in the daytime, but he was a friend of the world at night.

Samson's name means "man of the sun," from the Hebrew *shemesh* ("sun"). God intended for Samson's light to shine brightly like the sun. Instead, Samson ends up in darkness, blinded by the very enemies he was sent to defeat.

I remind you of a principle I mentioned at the beginning of this book. It is a principle of historical cycles running throughout the book of Judges.

- *Step 1*: God's people become complacent in their peace and prosperity, so they compromise their faith.
- *Step 2*: The Lord hands them over to oppressors.
- *Step 3*: God's people cry to him for deliverance.
- *Step 4*: God raises a judge to deliver them.
- *Step 5*: The cycle begins all over again.

And here's the most important part of this principle to remember: with each revolution of the cycle, there is a downward spiral. When it comes full circle, we are not back where we started. We have descended a notch lower toward cultural decline and destruction. Every time God's people compromise their faith, they become more wicked and depraved than the previous time.

Even the judges themselves seem to spiral downward, morally and spiritually, as we move through the narrative. We see no fatal moral defect in such judges as Ehud, Shamgar, or Deborah. Then we come to Gideon—a heroic and godly figure throughout most of his life, until he experiences a moral and spiritual collapse near the end. Finally, as we come to Samson, we find a man who is God's choice as judge and deliverer of Israel, and he is spiritually foolish and morally reprehensible throughout his life. He is a reflection of the corruption of his culture.

If one sentence summarizes the book of Judges, it is the statement in Judges 17:6 and repeated in 21:25—"In those days there was no king in Israel. Everyone did what was right in his own eyes." Samson was the ultimate example of this tragic attitude.

And just as Samson, the judge and deliver of Israel, was a

reflection of the culture of his day, all too many Christian leaders today reflect their culture more than they reflect the character and values of Jesus Christ.

Dead fish float with the stream. You never see a dead fish swimming upstream; they always float downstream. And a Christian leader who is not spiritually alive, who is not animated by the quickening Spirit of God and committed to the authority of the Word of God, is going to float downstream. He is not going to fight his way against the pressure of a corrupt culture, false doctrine, universalism, political correctness, moral relativism, cultural decay, and the now very popular stance of approving homosexuality. A spiritually dead Christian leader will float with the current, even if he has thousands attending his church.

Everywhere we look, we see so-called Christian leaders who are the moral equivalent of Samson. We see people who claim to stand for Christ, yet they are merely pale reflections of the surrounding culture. To stand for Christ is to stand against the culture. To be a friend of God is to be an enemy of the world. As Israel descended down that slippery slope into sin and corruption, even God's chosen deliverers, called to be reformers of the culture, partook in the sin of their culture. And we are seeing the same pattern played out in our culture today.

Living in Philistine Times

I would encourage you to read Judges 9 through 13. Rather than quote these passages, I will simply summarize.

In Judges 9, we read of the conspiracy of Gideon's son, Abimelech. In Judges 10, God raises up two deliverers, Tola and Jair, to deliver Israel. But the nation soon slides back into disobedience and oppression. In Judges 11, God raises up Jephthah as Israel's deliverer, yet he makes a foolish vow that proves disastrous for himself and his daughter, his only child. Judges 12 gives us compressed accounts of three lesser-known judges: Ibzan, Elon, and Abdon. And in Judges 13, we read of the birth of Samson.

At the time of Samson's birth, the heart of the nation of Israel was hardened by sin. For forty years, the nation had been occupied and oppressed by the Philistines. Israel had become so depraved and corrupt by this time that the people didn't even cry out to God for deliverance. They simply accepted the oppression of the Philistines. Israel had hit rock bottom. When a nation experiences such an intense level of pain and suffering, yet is so spiritually and morally dead that the people accept their oppression, that nation has sunk as low as it can go.

As I read Judges 13, I can't help but think of my own nation, my own culture. In earlier times, when America went through an experience such as a civil war, a world war, or the Great Depression, people would turn to God. They would repent of their sins. They would return to their houses of worship and seek God's mercy for their lives.

For a brief time after the 9/11 terror attacks, when people saw two of the world's tallest skyscrapers crumble into dust and flame, when they saw the Pentagon, the headquarters of America's military, suffer a surprise attack, people turned to God—for a few weeks, at least. But it wasn't long before complacency set in. Soon, life returned to normal and the churches became half-empty. Even the economic crisis of 2008, which nearly collapsed the global economy, did not turn hearts back to God.

As a culture, we no longer worry about sin, much less cry out to God for mercy. Our movies and TV shows are drenched in immorality and godlessness. Many Christian leaders are addicted to Internet pornography. Our TV commercials use nudity and sexual innuendo to sell hamburgers—yet we do not complain to the networks or the advertisers. The horror of abortion-on-demand has sent our society hurtling down a slippery slope, so that we have now begun to rationalize infanticide, the starving of severely brain-damaged patients, and withholding medical care for the elderly. We don't ask God for deliverance from this culture of sin. We accept it. We shrug and say, "What can we do?"

So as we read the story of Samson and his decaying, declining culture, I urge you not to think of this as a quaint but largely irrelevant Bible tale for Sunday school children. It is an intensely pertinent story about the spiritual and moral corruption that pervades our society today. The oppression of the Philistines that we read about in these pages is with us today in the oppression of secularism, moral relativism, and the depraved values that dominate our entertainment media, educational institutions, and our government. We are living in Philistine times, in a post-Christian age. The story of Samson speaks to us more relevantly today than ever before.

In Judges 13, God, in his mercy, sends an angel to a barren woman among the Israelites. The angel tells her, "Behold, you are barren and have not borne children, but you shall conceive and bear a son" (13:3). And he gives the woman special instructions regarding the pregnancy, because her son will be set apart for God from the womb, and he will deliver Israel from the oppression of the Philistines.

This woman, the mother of Samson, was unable to conceive a child by natural means. In order to have a child, she needed supernatural intervention. Her barrenness was a reflection of Israel's spiritual barrenness and moral fruitlessness. Israel needed supernatural intervention in order to be delivered from this state of spiritual emptiness.

The angel promised this woman that her son would be a Nazirite. The Hebrew word *nāzîr* means "consecrated" or "set aside." Those of the Nazirite order were set aside for God's purpose. God's laws concerning the Nazirites are found in Numbers 6 and contain three basic requirements:

1. A Nazirite must not eat or drink anything that comes from the grapevine.

2. A Nazirite must never touch a dead body, whether human or animal, lest he be defiled.

3. A Nazirite must never cut his hair.

As we examine the story of Samson, you will see that Samson broke all three of these vows.

And here we come to a common misunderstanding about Samson and his famous strength. Many people mistakenly believe that Samson's hair was the secret of his strength. That's not true. His hair was the *symbol* of his strength, but the *secret* of his strength was the Holy Spirit of God.

It's also important to note that Samson was a loner. You never see him in the company of the Israelite army. You never see him sitting down with a council of wise advisors and mentors. You never see him going to the tabernacle and asking for godly wisdom from the high priest. You never see him asking a friend to challenge his way of life and hold him accountable. Samson seems to think he doesn't need anyone in his life to help him live righteously and faithfully before God.

So for twenty years, Samson plays the role of champion of Israel. He is a hero with feet of clay. He is a strong leader, but not a godly leader. A godly leader can certainly be strong, but many strong leaders are far from godly. The difference between a strong leader and a godly leader is teachability. Samson was arrogant, self-satisfied, and self-confident, and he didn't think he needed to be taught about God and godliness. He was a man of faith, but he was not a faithful man, and it was his unfaithfulness that ultimately cost him his freedom, his sight, and his life.

Near the end of Judges 13, we read: "And the woman bore a son and called his name Samson. And the young man grew, and the LORD blessed him" (13:24). In Judges 14, we will see what Samson did with the Lord's blessings.

Stay Out of Timnah

Wherever you are on the spiritual scale—and we are all at different stages in our spiritual growth and maturity—there is a word from the Lord for you in Judges 14. It doesn't matter if you have known the Lord for sixty years or sixty minutes, there is a word from the Lord for you in this passage. No matter what you might have done, no matter how grievous your past sins, you will find strong encouragement in this passage, which speaks to us of the grace and overruling mercy of God.

Turning to Judges 14, we find that Samson has reached young adulthood:

> Samson went down to Timnah, and at Timnah he saw one of the daughters of the Philistines. Then he came up and told his father and mother, "I saw one of the daughters of the Philistines at Timnah. Now get her for me as my wife." But his father and mother said to him, "Is there not a woman among the daughters of your relatives, or among all our people, that you must go to take a wife from the uncircumcised Philistines?" But Samson

said to his father, "Get her for me, for she is right in my eyes."

His father and mother did not know that it was from the LORD, for he was seeking an opportunity against the Philistines. At that time the Philistines ruled over Israel (14:1-4).

There is not one Christian believer in the world today who can accurately say, "God cannot use me." God specializes in forgiveness, restoration, and reinstatement. Samson's weakness and failure are summarized in the first verse: "Samson went down to Timnah" (that's his first great failure) "and at Timnah he saw one of the daughters of the Philistines" (that's his second great failure).

I don't know what your Timnah is, but everybody has one, and I want to speak to you candidly about your Timnah: Be careful where you go. Be careful about placing yourself in situations of temptation. Be careful not to place yourself in situations where you might compromise your virtue, your moral principles, your faithfulness, or your Christian witness.

We know that Samson lived in the Hebrew village of Mahaneh-dan, between Zorah and Eshtaol, in the region of the tribe of Dan, next door to the region of Philistia. The Philistine village of Timnah was a mere four miles away (archaeologists have located the site of Timnah at modern-day Tel Batash in the Sorek Valley of Israel). So it was a very short walk from Samson's village to the Philistine village of Timnah.

For many Christians today, Timnah is a short drive to a place we shouldn't be, or a short walk next door, or a quick stroll to the next cubicle at the office. Our Timnah might be the touch of a button on the TV remote, or a few mouse clicks on the computer, or a few taps on a touch screen. Each of us has a Timnah, and we can all rationalize flirting with temptation. We tell ourselves, *It's okay to get close to temptation as long as I don't yield. I'm just going to look around. I won't do anything wrong.* But before you know it, you find yourself in Timnah, ensnared by a Philistine woman.

Many of us are like Samson—we are people of faith, but we are not faithful. We have faith in God, but we are not faithful to him in the way we live. We have faith in God, but we are not faithful with our eyes, with our words, with our actions, with our money, with the things we do when no one else is watching.

Samson was not faithful toward his Nazirite vows. He was not faithful in obeying the Word of God. He was not faithful to his parents' warnings and advice. They gave him excellent advice about not becoming romantically entangled with a pagan woman, a nonbeliever. They anticipated the sound New Testament counsel of the apostle Paul: "Do not be unequally yoked with unbelievers. For what partnership has righteousness with lawlessness? Or what fellowship has light with darkness?" (2 Corinthians 6:14).

But Samson, in his self-willed, unfaithful mindset, refused to listen to the advice of his parents. He was arrogantly convinced that he knew better than they did. So he took a four-mile walk from his village to the Philistine village of Timnah to see what he could see.

I have talked to many young people who have told me essentially the same story: "My parents don't understand that it's only a date. They're getting all upset over nothing. It's not as if I'm planning to marry this person. I just want to go out and have a good time. I would never marry a non-Christian. But there's nothing wrong with dating a non-Christian."

In all too many cases, that rationalization (which sounds so reasonable on the surface) leads to heartache and damaged lives. Initially, it's just a date. But soon attraction takes over, and once two people are attracted to each other, it becomes almost impossible for them to think rationally, logically, and biblically about the relationship. It's almost impossible for a Christian, in the throes of attraction, to think, *I'm feeling strong emotions, but I know that God's Word warns me not to be unequally yoked, so I'm just going to do the godly thing and end this relationship.* That almost never happens. Instead, people invent one rationalization after another to convince themselves that God's Word doesn't apply to this situation.

That's why it's so important not to place ourselves in situations of temptation. That's why the principle of not being unequally yoked applies not only to marriage but to dating, business and career relationships, interfaith efforts with non-Christians, and other relationships that could compromise our Christian principles and Christian witness.

This doesn't mean we are never to have anything to do with unbelievers. We can't be witnesses and salt and light unless we have friendships with unbelievers. But we need to know where to draw the line. Certain kinds of relationships entail the danger of becoming unequally yoked. We need to know the danger signs. We need to stay out of Timnah. Those who disobey God's warnings will inevitably inflict hurt and regret on themselves and others.

The Price of Disobedience

God will often overrule our disobedience and bring something good out of our moral and spiritual failures, just as he did in the life of Samson. If you date and marry an unbeliever, God may, at some point, after enormous suffering and pain, bring that unbelieving spouse to a place of belief. God may redeem a situation that should never have happened in the first place. But that doesn't mean there won't be a terrible price to pay in sorrow and regret.

God, in his sovereign wisdom, overruled the disobedience of Samson, and he actually used Samson's foolishness and disobedience to achieve his own purpose, which was to deliver Israel from the Philistines. But Samson paid a horrifying price for his willful disobedience of God, as we'll see in a moment.

Are you willing to pay such a price for disobedience? Whenever you put yourself in a situation where you force God to intervene to rescue you, whenever you think, *I'm going to sin, and God in his grace will clean up after my mess and make it all come out okay*, that's called "tempting God" or "putting God to the test." Tempting God through disobedience always results in suffering. God has promised to forgive us, but he has never promised to remove the natural consequences of our sin.

When Satan tempted Jesus, he took Jesus to the highest pinnacle of the temple and told him to leap off, and God the Father would send angels to save him. But Jesus replied, "You shall not put the Lord your God to the test" (Luke 4:12). In the New King James Version, it's rendered, "You shall not tempt the LORD your God." Never disobey God, and then expect God to rescue you from your own sinful foolishness. You'll regret it every time.

Two statements in this passage deserve closer examination. In Judges 14:3, after Samson's parents urge Samson to seek a wife from among the Israelites, Samson replies, "Get her for me, for she is right in my eyes." Samson is blunt and demanding to the point of rudeness toward his parents, and he makes a very telling statement: "for she is right in my eyes." In 14:7, Samson goes to Timnah and talks with the Philistine woman, and the text says again, "and she was right in Samson's eyes." Notice that these words echo the statement found in Judges 17:6 and 21:25—"In those days there was no king in Israel. Everyone did what was right in his own eyes."

This Philistine woman was not right in God's eyes, but Samson cared only about what was right in his own eyes—and the Philistine woman appealed to Samson's eyes. Though it is subtly stated, this indicates how self-willed Samson was. He made demands of his parents and he ignored the commandments of God. It tells us how much Samson reflected the decline of Israelite culture in that day.

The second statement that deserves our attention is in Judges 14:4—"His father and mother did not know that it was from the LORD, for he was seeking an opportunity against the Philistines. At that time the Philistines ruled over Israel." This doesn't mean that God approved of Samson's actions. When the text says "it was from the LORD," it means that God was going to use Samson's corrupt motives and disobedience to achieve his divine goal, which was the overthrow of Philistine oppression.

We see a similar principle in Joshua 11:20, where we read, "For it was the LORD's doing to harden their hearts that they should come against Israel in battle, in order that they should be devoted to destruction and should receive no mercy but be destroyed, just as the LORD commanded Moses." It was sinful for the enemies of Israel to devote themselves to destroying God's people, yet God chose to give them over to the hardening of their hearts so that they would be destroyed and would trouble Israel no more.

God will work with whatever we give him. If we are humble, faithful, and obedient, he will work with our faithfulness, and we will receive the blessing and reward for serving God. If we are arrogant, unfaithful, and disobedient, he will work with our waywardness to achieve his purpose, but instead of blessing, we will receive the natural consequences of sin.

Samson's March Toward Sin

God called Samson to be a judge and deliverer of Israel—and Samson's purpose in life was to liberate Israel from oppression by the Philistines. So Samson should have been at war with the enemies of God, the enemies of Israel, the Philistine nation. Instead, he went to a Philistine wedding. The details of the story are significant:

> Then Samson went down with his father and mother to Timnah, and they came to the vineyards of Timnah. And behold, a young lion came toward him roaring. Then the Spirit of the LORD rushed upon him, and although he had nothing in his hand, he tore the lion in pieces as one tears a young goat. But he did not tell his father or his mother what he had done. Then he went down and talked with the woman, and she was right in Samson's eyes.

> After some days he returned to take her. And he turned aside to see the carcass of the lion, and behold, there was a swarm of bees in the body of the lion, and honey. He scraped it out into his hands and went on, eating as he went. And he came to his father and mother and gave some to them, and they ate. But he did not tell them that he had scraped the honey from the carcass of the lion (Judges 14:5-9).

Casual readers might miss the fact that Samson broke at least one and most likely two of his three Nazirite vows in these verses. When Samson went into the vineyard, he probably ate some grapes, thus breaking his first vow not to eat or drink anything that comes from the grapevine. For a Nazirite to go into a vineyard was like a recovering alcoholic going to a wine-tasting party. Samson had no business being in the vineyard.

While Samson was in the vineyard, God sent a lion to him as a warning. The passage tells us, "Then the Spirit of the LORD rushed upon him, and although he had nothing in his hand, he tore the lion in pieces as one tears a young goat" (14:6). Samson withstood the attack of the lion and killed it. Yet, even after this warning from God, Samson persisted in his march toward Timnah, toward sin and disobedience.

A few weeks later, Samson went to claim his bride, against the advice of his godly parents. He went to the vineyard and turned aside to find the lion's carcass (to glory in his prowess, no doubt), and he found bees swarming in the carcass. The bees had made a honeycomb in the carcass, so Samson scraped out some honey with his hands and ate it to nourish himself on his journey.

When Samson scraped honey from the lion's carcass, he broke his second vow. As a Nazirite, he was sworn never to touch a dead body of either a human being or an animal. He broke these two vows without any apparent twinge of conscience. Breaking his vows didn't bother him, because he simply did what was right in his own eyes.

A Deadly Riddle

One of the lessons of the life of Samson is that we as parents and leaders must teach the next generation how to stand firmly against temptation and the enemies of Christ. Samson flirted with temptation and fraternized with the enemy. By setting himself up for failure, Samson became his own worst enemy. The story continues:

His father went down to the woman, and Samson prepared a feast there, for so the young men used to do. As soon as the people saw him, they brought thirty companions to be with him. And Samson said to them, "Let me now put a riddle to you. If you can tell me what it is, within the seven days of the feast, and find it out, then I will give you thirty linen garments and thirty changes of clothes, but if you cannot tell me what it is, then you shall give me thirty linen garments and thirty changes of clothes." And they said to him, "Put your riddle, that we may hear it." And he said to them,

"Out of the eater came something to eat.
Out of the strong came something sweet."

And in three days they could not solve the riddle.

On the fourth day they said to Samson's wife, "Entice your husband to tell us what the riddle is, lest we burn you and your father's house with fire. Have you invited us here to impoverish us?" (Judges 14:10-15).

As custom dictated, Samson prepared a feast, a bachelor party. Whenever the Bible speaks of a feast, wine is served. Did Samson break his vow by imbibing the wine? The text does not tell us, but from all we know about Samson and the ease with which he broke his other vows, it seems unlikely that he would be the only one at the party without a drink in his hand.

In the course of the party, Samson constructed a riddle. In the Hebrew language, the riddle rhymed, and the translators of the English Standard Version preserved this sense by rendering Samson's riddle as a rhyming couplet: "Out of the eater came something to eat. / Out of the strong came something sweet."

Samson's riddle tells us something about the mindset of this man. Remember, he is constructing the riddle out of his experience with sin. When he took the honey out of the lion's carcass, he was breaking his Nazirite vow. Samson should have been ashamed of his sin. He should have mourned the breaking of his vow. Instead, he made a joke of it. How insensitive to sin can one man be?

As a riddle, it was completely unfair. Unless you had actually seen Samson scooping honey out of the carcass of the lion, how could you possibly figure out the riddle? The Philistines tried and tried to solve it, without success.

Ancient wedding celebrations lasted for seven days and ended with the bride and groom going off together to consummate the marriage. The Philistines spent the first three days trying to figure out the answer to Samson's riddle. Finally, the enraged Philistines turned on Samson's bride and threatened to kill her and her family with fire if she didn't give them the secret of the riddle. The next few verses tell us what Samson's bride did next:

> And Samson's wife wept over him and said, "You only hate me; you do not love me. You have put a riddle to my people, and you have not told me what it is." And he said to her, "Behold, I have not told my father nor my mother, and shall I tell you?" She wept before him the seven days that their feast lasted, and on the seventh day he told her, because she pressed him hard. Then she told the riddle to her people. And the men of the city said to him on the seventh day before the sun went down,
>
> "What is sweeter than honey?
> What is stronger than a lion?"
>
> And he said to them,

> "If you had not plowed with my heifer,
> you would not have found out my riddle."

And the Spirit of the LORD rushed upon him, and he went down to Ashkelon and struck down thirty men of the town and took their spoil and gave the garments to those who had told the riddle. In hot anger he went back to his father's house. And Samson's wife was given to his companion, who had been his best man (Judges 14:16-20).

Samson's bride begged, nagged, pouted, wheedled, cajoled, and pestered Samson from the fourth day to the seventh day of the wedding celebration, trying to get him to reveal the answer to the riddle. She tried every trick in the book, accusing Samson of not loving her and even breaking down in tears. The fact that Samson relented and gave her the information on the final day of the marriage celebration suggests that she may have ultimately threatened not to consummate the marriage.

As strong as he was, Samson was no match for the constant pressure and tears of this pagan woman. She was fighting for her life and the life of her family, and she would stop at nothing to break Samson down. She enticed him, she defeated him, and finally, she betrayed him.

Samson is a picture of what the world does to people of faith who are unfaithful. He is an object lesson in how the world breaks the resistance of a compromising Christian. Someone has observed that Samson could tear a lion in half with his bare hands and slay an army with a donkey's jawbone, but he was no match for the tears of the Philistine woman.

As a result, the wedding feast became a mass funeral for thirty

Philistine men. A joyful celebration turned to mourning. Samson never got to consummate his marriage. The Philistines gave his bride away to his best man.

Whenever we flirt with temptation and compromise with sin, we bring about sorrow and suffering in our own lives and the lives of many others. The consequences of our sin may not appear immediately, but they cannot be escaped. As Bible teacher Charles Haddon Spurgeon once observed, "God will not allow His children to sin successfully."[35]

As painful as it was for Samson to have his marriage annulled, it would have been worse had the marriage gone forward. God's purpose for Samson's life—delivering Israel from the Philistine oppression—would have been derailed. This doesn't mean that God's plan would have been thwarted. His will cannot be nullified. God would have simply accomplished his will by a different means. But if Samson had become unequally yoked with a Philistine woman, he might have lost the opportunity of being used by God as Israel's deliverer.

An Exclusive Faith

Nothing but sorrow comes from insisting on our own agenda instead of God's agenda. His Word calls us to a narrow and exclusive path.

God said that we are to love him exclusively and have no other gods besides him. Jesus said that he alone is the way, the truth, and the life, and there is no other way to God the Father but through Jesus exclusively. The Scriptures tell us that Christian marriage is exclusive, and that we should marry only another believer. The Scriptures also tell us that Christian morality is exclusive and that sexual relations should take place only within a holy and heterosexual marriage. The

Bible also tells us that God's truth is absolute and exclusive, and that anything that contradicts God's Word is not truth.

So here is the tension: Christianity is a highly exclusive faith—but the culture we live in abhors exclusivity. Our secular culture calls Christians "hateful" because we are not inclusive. Our secular culture hates us for saying that Jesus is the only way to God the Father, that there is only one path to heaven, that Christians should not be unequally yoked with non-Christians, and that same-sex marriage is a sin. Our secular culture hates us for saying that abortion is the killing of a human life and not simply a choice.

That's why relativism and personal autonomy are so popular in our culture today. "Truth" is whatever is true for you. You are free to believe that there are many roads to God, that God can be defined in any way we wish (including as gods and goddesses and even demons), that inclusiveness toward sexual immorality and abortion is a good thing, and on and on.

The secularists hate us for being "judgmental." But the Bible calls us to use good moral judgment and to hold our society accountable for violating God's laws. When you do that, people with poor judgment and no respect for God's laws are bound to call you judgmental. But we must not allow godless people to intimidate us or dissuade us from doing the work God has called us to do.

We also need to understand that much of the opposition to a biblical worldview now comes from within so-called Christian or evangelical circles. Some Christian books, Christian speakers and preachers, and Christian churches preach worldly inclusiveness. They preach a gospel in which Jesus is just one way to the Father, not the only way. They preach a gospel in which biblical morality is intolerant and judgmental, and our true priority as Christians should not be evangelizing the world but saving the environment or serving a worldly political agenda.

One of the most libelous of all of Satan's lies is his smear of Christians as being hateful and intolerant. Those who follow the teachings of Jesus Christ are the most loving and genuinely tolerant people in the world. As Christians, we believe in Christlike love and acceptance of all people. We believe in serving the needs of the poor and hungry, the widows and orphans. In fact, Christians founded the first hospitals (in medieval France, a hospital was known as a hôtel-Dieu, "a hotel of God").

Christians led the fight to abolish slavery and segregation because our Bible tells us, "There is neither Jew nor Greek, there is neither slave nor free, there is no male and female, for you are all one in Christ Jesus" (Galatians 3:28), and "Accept one another, then, just as Christ accepted you, in order to bring praise to God" (Romans 15:7).

Yet the secularists and religious compromisers call us bigots because we insist on biblical morality. In order to bring more young people into the church, many compromising churches preach an unbiblical universalism and soft-pedal the exclusive truth of the Christian gospel. Many shallow-minded sloganeers in the church now say, "Love unites; doctrine divides."

Well, as Paul writes in Ephesians 4:15, we must speak the truth in love—*but we must speak the truth*. And sometimes the truth divides because *truth is exclusive*. Sin does not equal righteousness any more than $2 + 2 = 5$.

The compromisers in the church claim that if we proclaim an exclusive gospel, we will alienate the culture. I don't want to alienate non-Christians. I love non-Christians. I gladly serve non-Christians.

But let's be clear: We cannot love and serve non-Christians by suppressing the truth and denying what the Scriptures teach. We don't do non-Christians any favors by substituting a diluted and contaminated gospel in place of true living water. If we sell out the truth in order to attract non-Christians into our churches, what do we really offer them?

Yes, if we speak the truth, we risk alienating some non-Christians. But if we compromise the truth, we will alienate our Lord and Savior, Jesus Christ. That is the choice that confronts us, and it is a stark and exclusive choice.

When the chips are down and you must decide, who will you choose to alienate?

8

The Danger
of Tempting God

Samson will always be remembered for his haircut. It was the most expensive haircut in human history. It cost him everything. He will also be remembered for his immoral lifestyle—and for the tragic consequences of his immorality.

I said in the previous chapter that I find Samson to be a depressing character to study. It saddens me to read about his life because he is a man with so much potential, a man so gifted by God, yet he squandered those gifts on a reckless and immoral lifestyle.

Samson was a living paradox. Here was a brave man who could tear a lion in half with his bare hands, yet he could not control himself. His enemies could not bind him because he could break any fetters they placed on him, yet he ended up blinded and imprisoned by his uncontrolled appetite for sin.

The apostle Paul reminds us that we should be warned and

instructed by the tragic moral failures of Old Testament people like Samson:

> Now these things took place as examples for us, that we might not desire evil as they did. Do not be idolaters as some of them were; as it is written, "The people sat down to eat and drink and rose up to play." We must not indulge in sexual immorality as some of them did, and twenty-three thousand fell in a single day…Now these things happened to them as an example, but they were written down for our instruction, on whom the end of the ages has come. Therefore let anyone who thinks that he stands take heed lest he fall. No temptation has overtaken you that is not common to man. God is faithful, and he will not let you be tempted beyond your ability, but with the temptation he will also provide the way of escape, that you may be able to endure it (1 Corinthians 10:6-8,11-13).

Samson's life is a warning to all of us. As we train the next generation, we should hold up the story of Samson as Exhibit A—the evidence of what happens to a person of faith who does not live faithfully, a servant of God who serves his own lusts and animal instincts. The story of Samson is an antidote to the spiritual amnesia so epidemic in our culture and our churches. Times change, but spiritual principles are timeless. The same God who repeatedly delivered the Israelites when they cried out to him will deliver us from temptation today.

The English reformer and martyr John Bradford (1510–1555) was imprisoned in the Tower of London by order of Queen Mary I ("Bloody Mary") for the crime of being a Protestant. While Bradford was in the Tower, he would see other criminals being led away to their execution—men who were condemned for such crimes as murder, rape, and robbery. Bradford was grateful to God that he was imprisoned for his faith and not for any crime. When he saw a condemned criminal going to his death, he would say, "There, but for the grace of God, goes John Bradford." On July 1, 1555, Bradford was led away from his cell and burned at the stake, a martyr for Jesus Christ.

Whenever I hear about a Christian leader who has yielded to temptation and has morally fallen, I am reminded of those words of John Bradford, and I think, *There, but for the grace of God, go I.* We are all human, fallen, and subject to temptation. The lesson of Samson's life is that we must be continually on our guard against the temptations and enticements that seek to destroy us.

It's often said that God has a wonderful plan for your life, and it's true. He does. But we must never forget that Satan has a plan for our lives too. He is continually scheming to destroy our lives and neutralize our witness for God. If you are a genuine worshiper of the Lord Jesus Christ, Satan and his demons will tempt you to your own destruction. That's why the apostle Peter writes, "Be sober-minded; be watchful. Your adversary the devil prowls around like a roaring lion, seeking someone to devour" (1 Peter 5:8).

What Was Right in His Own Eyes

At the end of Judges 14, we saw that Samson's Philistine wife, fearing the threats of the other Philistines to burn her and her family to death, coaxed Samson into revealing the answer to his riddle. She passed the answer along to the Philistines, and they mocked Samson with the answer before the sun went down on the seventh day of the wedding celebration: "What is sweeter than honey?" they said. "What is stronger than a lion?" (14:18).

Enraged, Samson traveled about twenty miles to the Philistine town of Ashkelon, where he killed thirty Philistine men and took their clothes to pay off the wager over his riddle. Then he went back home to his father's house, only to discover later that his father-in-law had taken his bride and given her to the best man.

Judges 15 continues the story. Even though Samson's wife has been given to another man, he still considers her his wife. He goes to her, taking a young goat as a peace offering, with the intention of consummating the marriage. Her father, however, will not allow him to see his wife. He tells Samson, "I really thought that you utterly hated her, so I gave her to your companion. Is not her younger sister more beautiful than she? Please take her instead."

But Samson won't have it. He decides to take out his anger toward his father-in-law against all the Philistine people and do as much harm to them as he can. So he catches three hundred foxes, ties them tail to tail, attaches a torch to their tails, and lets them loose in the Philistine grain fields and orchards, destroying their crops.

In doing so, Samson triggers a cycle of revenge. The Philistines respond by going to the home of Samson's in-laws, and they burn Samson's wife and father-in-law to death. So Samson, predictably enough, swears vengeance on the Philistines. He viciously attacks a group of Philistines, slaughtering many of them, and then he runs off and hides in a cave.

The Philistines, eager for the next round of revenge, raid a settlement of the Israelite tribe of Judah (Samson is of the neighboring tribe of Dan). The men of Judah, who had been trying to keep peace with the Philistines, go to Samson and say, "Do you not know that the Philistines are rulers over us? What then is this that you have done to us?" Sampson replied with childish logic: "As they did to me, so have I done to them." The men of Judah offer a deal: they will bind Samson with ropes and hand him over to the Philistines, but they will not harm him themselves. Samson agrees to the arrangement.

When the men of Judah turn Samson over to the Philistines, the Philistines shout with joy and rush upon Samson, intending to take their revenge on him. With a shrug, Samson easily breaks the ropes that bind him. He snatches up the jawbone of a donkey, wields it like a sword, and uses it to strike down a thousand Philistines.

After this defeat, the Philistines don't dare to attack Samson for a long time. Judges 15 closes with the statement, "And he judged Israel in the days of the Philistines twenty years" (15:20). The tragedy of Samson's life is that he reflected the brutal spirit of his times rather than the wise Spirit of God. He was vengeful, lustful, self-willed, and quick to anger. Like the people of Israel in the time of the judges, he did what was right in his own eyes.

Birds Nesting in Your Hair

Samson never seemed to struggle against temptation. Instead, he seemed to yield to every impulse, whether a lustful impulse, an impulse for revenge, or an impulse for violence. His unwillingness to govern and resist his impulses continually placed him in situations of conflict and sexual temptation.

As Christians, as civilized human beings, we have to govern our impulses. We have to resist temptation. Any person today who, in a fit of jealous rage, committed random acts of arson and slaughter as Samson did would soon find himself behind bars.

You may be thinking, *I'll never end up like Samson. His story has no relevance to my life.* Yet I have spoken with many Christians who were once as strong and committed to their faith as you are—yet they fell to the same temptations Samson fell to. Remember the warning of Paul: "Therefore let anyone who thinks that he stands take heed lest he fall" (1 Corinthians 10:12).

We cannot turn off temptation, but Paul tells us we can live victoriously over temptation. "God is faithful," he continues, "and he will not let you be tempted beyond your ability" (10:13). But if that's true, why does temptation so often win?

A large part of the answer lies in the fact that we have not fully surrendered our will to Christ. We have human free will, given to us by God, and the only way to defeat temptation is to surrender our will to him. As long as we remain self-willed, we will continually tempt ourselves and follow our own selfish lusts.

We know that Satan tempts us, but we fail to realize that we often tempt ourselves. We are often our own worst enemies. We see this principle again and again in the life of Samson. Martin Luther put it this way: "I cannot stop the bird from flying over my head, but I can certainly stop it from nesting in my hair." Samson clearly enjoyed having birds nest in his hair—and tragically, so do many of us.

When Jesus taught us to pray, "Lead us not into temptation" (Matthew 6:13), he was actually teaching us to ask God to empower us not to tempt ourselves. Another way of putting it would be, "Help me not to let the birds of temptation nest in my hair. Remind me to stay out of situations of temptation."

Whenever the subject of temptation comes up, most people think of sexual temptation, whether it is sex outside of marriage, or a pornography habit, or thoughts of lust. These are real temptations that can destroy your relationships, your life, and your witness for Christ. But the realm of temptation is much broader than sexual temptation. We are tempted in many ways toward many different kinds of sin.

We are tempted to whittle down our tithes and offerings to our leftover pocket change instead of the firstfruits of our labors. We are tempted to waste time and energy on mindless entertainment or surfing the Internet or fiddling with our smartphones instead of spending our precious time serving God, enjoying our families, and teaching and loving our children. We are tempted to cut ethical corners in our careers. We are tempted to lose emotional control, to vent our anger and frustration on other people, and to treat people in ways that are anything but Christlike. We are tempted to disregard the feelings and thoughts of others and to engage in behavior that, while not strictly forbidden in Scripture, might compromise our witness and offend a weaker Christian.

God never tempts anyone, but we often tempt God and tempt ourselves. As we discussed in the previous chapter, whenever you place yourself in circumstances where your only hope is for God to rescue you, it's called "tempting God" or "putting God to the test." Though God freely forgives our sin, he has never promised to remove the natural consequences that come with sin. So tempting God brings harm to our lives that often cannot be undone.

Samson repeatedly tempted God so that his only hope was for God to continually deliver him from foolishness and sin. After rescuing Samson again and again, God finally gave him over to the consequences of his lust and folly. The life of Samson is proof of the wise words of King Solomon:

> My son, be attentive to my wisdom;
>   incline your ear to my understanding,
> that you may keep discretion,
>   and your lips may guard knowledge.
> For the lips of a forbidden woman drip honey,
>   and her speech is smoother than oil,

> but in the end she is bitter as wormwood,
>   sharp as a two-edged sword.
> Her feet go down to death;
>   her steps follow the path to Sheol.
>   (Proverbs 5:1-5)

In Judges 14, we saw how Samson tempted God when he went to Timnah, four miles from his home. The result of Samson's choice was suffering for many people, including himself. Everything that happened was the result of Samson's refusal to heed God's warnings. Samson tempted God and he tempted himself.

Now, in Judges 16, Samson really goes out of his way to disobey God. Instead of traveling a mere four miles from home, Samson travels to Gaza—ten times the distance to Timnah. There is an important principle in this account: If you don't stop at four miles, you will end up going forty miles. If you don't stop at Timnah, you'll end up in Gaza.

What Happens in Gaza

Today, Gaza City is a Palestinian city in the Gaza Strip (the Palestinians proudly consider themselves direct descendants of the Philistines). The city has been inhabited for thirty-five hundred years and was ruled by ancient Egypt before becoming one of the five chief cities of the Philistines (the Philistine Pentapolis consisted of Ashkelon, Ashdod, Ekron, Gath, and Gaza). The city of Gaza later came under the rule of the Romans, the Byzantines, the Islamic Rashidun army, and the Crusaders. Gaza was raided by Mongols, incorporated into the Ottoman Empire, absorbed by the British Mandate of Palestine during World War I, administered by Egypt after the 1948 Arab-Israeli War, captured by Israel in the 1967 Six-Day War, and transferred to the Palestinian National Authority in

1993. Currently controlled by the Palestinian Sunni Islamic resistance movement Hamas, Gaza City is a source of international tensions to this day.

In the time of Samson, the city of Gaza was much like Las Vegas in our time—except that what happened in Gaza didn't stay in Gaza. When you are God's man but you yield yourself to immorality, people will find out and word will spread. In Judges 16, we read:

> Samson went to Gaza, and there he saw a prostitute, and he went in to her. The Gazites were told, "Samson has come here." And they surrounded the place and set an ambush for him all night at the gate of the city. They kept quiet all night, saying, "Let us wait till the light of the morning; then we will kill him" (16:1-2).

These Philistines knew that Samson was the judge of Israel. They remembered that this Israelite, armed with nothing by the jawbone of a donkey, had slaughtered a thousand Philistine warriors. So they gathered around the house of the prostitute where Samson stayed— and they waited for him to come out.

When you are blessed by God in your business, your possessions, your career, or your family, you are at a dangerous point. Whenever you are blessed by God, it is time to take extra spiritual precautions.

In times of blessing and prosperity, people begin to think, *God is blessing me, so what I do inwardly and secretly must not be important to God. Other people are suffering, but I'm not. God must be pleased with me, he must favor me. He winks at my sins. I can do no wrong.* Once we tell ourselves our hidden sins don't matter to God, we are setting ourselves up for a big fall.

This kind of thinking got Samson into trouble. He repeatedly used God's strength for his own purposes. He repeatedly used God's blessings to cover up for his own sins. He became arrogant and self-satisfied. *God must be really pleased with me*, Samson probably thought to himself. *What I do with my private life doesn't matter to God. Nobody will ever know what I did here in Gaza. What happens in Gaza stays in Gaza, right?* Wrong. God cares about our lives, including our hidden sins.

Judges 16 begins, "Samson went to Gaza, and there he saw…" Notice that phrase: "he saw." This statement echoes verse 14:1, the first time Samson got into trouble: "Samson went down to Timnah, and at Timnah *he saw* one of the daughters of the Philistines." The role Samson's eyesight played in leading him astray is critical for us to understand. His eyes got him into trouble four miles from home in Timnah—and they got him into trouble forty miles from home in Gaza. As we will later see, when his enemies finally capture him, they gouge out his eyes.

What was Samson looking for when he went to the house of the prostitute? Was he seeking a wife? Was he looking for tender, romantic love? A caring relationship? A self-sacrificial commitment? No. Samson was looking for instant gratification.

Look around at our own society with spiritual eyes, and you will see people who are hungry and desperate to be loved and accepted. And all too often, they settle for sex. They want to be valued and esteemed, but they settle for being used as an object of momentary pleasure. They are made in God's image, and God himself has said that it's not good for people to be alone. Yet people settle for a counterfeit togetherness that ultimately leads to more emptiness and loneliness than ever.

God created safe enclosures where lonely people can find unity, love, acceptance, worth, and esteem. God created marriage as the safe enclosure for the sexual union between a man and a woman. God created the family as the safe enclosure for raising healthy children. God created the church, the community of faith, as the safe enclosure for Christian brothers and sisters to have fellowship together.

But the world offers its deceptive counterfeit for all of these safe enclosures. The world offers casual and promiscuous sex, prostitution, the emptiness of pornography, the sham of same-sex marriage, the corner bar as a substitute church, and the many anonymous pseudo-communities that exist on the Internet. People are hungry for unconditional love and acceptance—but they are chasing the mirage-like values of power, fame, money, and sex.

Our culture has abandoned God and the joy that comes from knowing God. The people around us, our neighbors and coworkers, have rejected the pure Living Water of spiritual refreshment in favor of the salty, polluted water that spews from our corrupt culture, producing endless thirst. As our civilization is dying of thirst, the Living Water cries out, "Come to me! Come to me! Drink and be satisfied!" For only in Jesus can you find your worth, your esteem, and unconditional love.

Samson, a man of faith who was unfaithful to God, sought instant gratification in the arms of a prostitute. And while he was in her house, Philistine men surrounded the house and prepared to ambush him when he came out.

> But Samson lay till midnight, and at midnight he arose and took hold of the doors of the gate of the city and the two posts, and pulled them up, bar and all, and put them on his shoulders and carried them to the top of the hill that is in front of Hebron (Judges 16:3).

This passage raises many questions in our minds: Why did Samson go to Gaza? Did he have to travel forty miles just to visit a prostitute? Why did he arise at midnight? When he went out of the house, why didn't the Philistines attack him? Why did Samson pull up the gate, and why carry it all the way to Hebron, a distance of forty miles?

Perhaps the Philistines were about to attack Samson—then they saw him rip the city gate out of the ground and carry it on his shoulders. The Philistines knew who Samson was and that's why they plotted against him. They knew that this man had slaughtered a thousand Philistines with the jawbone of a donkey, and it may well be that when they saw him yank up that gate as easily as a farmer pulling a radish out of the ground, their plans instantly changed.

In the Old Testament, the gates of the city are a symbol of the strength, prosperity, and power of that city. Strong city gates mean a well-protected city. Business and commerce were transacted at the gates of the city. He who possesses the city gates possesses the power to defeat the enemy.

That's why Jesus, in Matthew 16:18, said that the gates of hell could not defeat his followers, the church. Jesus was giving us a word picture of the church's victory over Satan. When Jesus rose from the grave, he shattered the gates of hell and gave us the victory. All we have to do to be victorious is to claim the Lord's victory over hell.

Samson used God's gift of supernatural strength for selfish purposes. He took God's grace and God's blessings for granted. When we squander the blessings of the Lord on our lusts, ambitions, and selfish impulses, neglecting to use God's blessings to serve his purpose and his agenda, we can be sure that a day of reckoning is coming. In fact, that day may already be here.

Though the book of Judges relates these events without

commentary, it may be significant that it was in the city of Gaza that Samson committed sin with the prostitute. Gaza is where Samson will be enslaved and his eyes gouged out.

The Temptress in the Valley

Satan knows he cannot *destroy* the believer because, as Jesus said, "I give them eternal life, and they will never perish, and no one will snatch them out of my hand" (John 10:28). But Satan delights in *defeating* the believer. We hand him the victory on a silver platter whenever we tempt ourselves into sin. Like the Philistines, Satan waits until we are mired deep in sin, then he moves in for the kill. But even when we fail, we are protected by the blood of Jesus Christ. We can overcome again and again through confession and sincere repentance.

God wants to take us from failure to victory. That's why he often shakes us awake and invites us to return to him. He generously restores us again and again. He overrules our failures and sins, and he urges us, through the voice of his Spirit, to learn from our sins and grow from our failures.

But if we persist in sin, as Samson did, God will ultimately allow us to drink the bitter water of the consequences of sin. And those consequences are often more painful and more deadly than we imagine.

The Philistines wanted to do to Samson what Satan wants to do to you and to me. They wanted to neutralize him and torment him. They wanted to neutralize his power and effectiveness for God. They wanted to negate his usefulness to God.

Because a believer is guarded by the hand of God for all eternity, Satan works day and night, 24/7, trying to lead you into sin and disgrace, trying to paralyze you with shame and doubt, trying to nullify

your testimony. Though Satan cannot destroy you, he can do the
next worst thing—he can render you useless for God's service.

After the Philistines tried repeatedly and unsuccessfully to
destroy Samson, they devised a plan to nullify and neutralize Samson and render him useless to God. The Philistine plan involved a
woman named Delilah:

> After this [Samson] loved a woman in the Valley of
> Sorek, whose name was Delilah. And the lords of the
> Philistines came up to her and said to her, "Seduce him,
> and see where his great strength lies, and by what means
> we may overpower him, that we may bind him to hum-
> ble him. And we will each give you 1,100 pieces of silver."
> So Delilah said to Samson, "Please tell me where your
> great strength lies, and how you might be bound, that
> one could subdue you."
>
> Samson said to her, "If they bind me with seven fresh
> bowstrings that have not been dried, then I shall become
> weak and be like any other man." Then the lords of the
> Philistines brought up to her seven fresh bowstrings that
> had not been dried, and she bound him with them. Now
> she had men lying in ambush in an inner chamber. And
> she said to him, "The Philistines are upon you, Samson!"
> But he snapped the bowstrings, as a thread of flax snaps
> when it touches the fire. So the secret of his strength was
> not known.
>
> Then Delilah said to Samson, "Behold, you have mocked
> me and told me lies. Please tell me how you might be
> bound." And he said to her, "If they bind me with new
> ropes that have not been used, then I shall become weak
> and be like any other man." So Delilah took new ropes

and bound him with them and said to him, "The Philistines are upon you, Samson!" And the men lying in
ambush were in an inner chamber. But he snapped the
ropes off his arms like a thread.

Then Delilah said to Samson, "Until now you have
mocked me and told me lies. Tell me how you might
be bound." And he said to her, "If you weave the seven
locks of my head with the web and fasten it tight with
the pin, then I shall become weak and be like any other
man." So while he slept, Delilah took the seven locks of
his head and wove them into the web. And she made
them tight with the pin and said to him, "The Philistines are upon you, Samson!" But he awoke from his
sleep and pulled away the pin, the loom, and the web.

And she said to him, "How can you say, 'I love you,'
when your heart is not with me? You have mocked me
these three times, and you have not told me where your
great strength lies." And when she pressed him hard with
her words day after day, and urged him, his soul was
vexed to death. And he told her all his heart, and said to
her, "A razor has never come upon my head, for I have
been a Nazirite to God from my mother's womb. If my
head is shaved, then my strength will leave me, and I
shall become weak and be like any other man" (Judges
16:4-17).

Delilah lived in the Valley of Sorek, the border between the Israelite tribe of Dan and the Philistine lands. The word *sorek* refers
to the grapes grown in that valley, which is still a grape- and wine-
producing region to this day.

Samson fell in love with Delilah. The Scriptures do not tell us that Delilah herself was a Philistine woman, but she willingly took money from the Philistine leaders, "the lords of the Philistines," to betray Samson.

It's unclear if Samson was arrogant, incredibly stupid, or addled by alcohol. Perhaps he was all of the above. In any case, Delilah repeatedly nagged him about the secret of his strength. To get her to stop nagging, he lied: "If the Philistines bind me with seven fresh bowstrings, I'll lose my strength." Or, "If they bind me with new ropes..." Or, "If you weave my hair in a certain way..."

Doesn't he notice that every time he tells Delilah a lie, the Philistines try that very method to entrap him? Isn't it obvious to him that Delilah is betraying him again and again? Why, then, does he stay with her? Why does he finally tell her the true secret of his strength? Again, it seems that Samson must have been overconfident or simply drunk.

When Delilah kept nagging Samson about his secret, he should have put on his sneakers and run. That, of course, is what Joseph did when Potiphar's wife tried to seduce him (see Genesis 39). If Samson had followed Joseph's example, he might have lost his cloak, but he would have kept his integrity, his hair, his eyes, his strength, and his usefulness to God.

The Betrayal

Now comes the moment of Delilah's ultimate betrayal of Samson—and Samson's tragic betrayal of himself:

> When Delilah saw that he had told her all his heart, she sent and called the lords of the Philistines, saying, "Come up again, for he has told me all his heart." Then the lords of the Philistines came up to her and brought the money in their hands. She made him sleep on her

knees. And she called a man and had him shave off the
seven locks of his head. Then she began to torment him,
and his strength left him. And she said, "The Philistines
are upon you, Samson!" And he awoke from his sleep
and said, "I will go out as at other times and shake myself
free." But he did not know that the LORD had left him.
And the Philistines seized him and gouged out his eyes
and brought him down to Gaza and bound him with
bronze shackles. And he ground at the mill in the prison.
But the hair of his head began to grow again after it had
been shaved (Judges 16:18-22).

Again, let's be clear on this: Samson's strength was not in his hair.
There was nothing magical about Samson's hair. It was merely a symbol of his Nazirite vow—the outward representation of an inward
obedience. It was an external sign of an internal covenant with God.

As we've already seen, Samson had previously broken his other
Nazirite vows. When we break our vows to God, we become weak-
ened spiritually. Samson had broken his vow to abstain from grapes.
He had broken his vow not to touch a corpse. But until he shared
his secret with Delilah, until she called in a man to cut off Samson's
hair, Samson had at least kept this one vow inviolate. Perhaps God
in his grace remained with Samson as long as he kept one of the
three vows, but when Samson awoke from his haircut, "he did not
know that the LORD had left him."

The secret of Samson's strength was the supernatural power of
God, poured out on him by the Holy Spirit. When the last shred
of his broken vows was stripped away, the power of God departed
from him.

Whenever I read the words of Judges 16:20, "he did not know
that the LORD had left him," as God is my witness, my knees shake.

I literally want to go down on my face before God, begging him to never let me fall into a state of self-deception like Samson's.

Imagine Samson's bewilderment as he hears Delilah say, "The Philistines are upon you, Samson!" And as he groggily awakens from his stupor, he says, "I will go out as at other times and shake myself free." He thinks he is strong, but he is defenseless. He doesn't realize the danger he is in. He doesn't realize the threat he faces. He doesn't know that the Lord's strength has left him.

The Scriptures are clear that the Lord will never leave us nor forsake us. But the Scriptures are equally clear that God's strength can depart from us when we persist in sin and disobedience. No wonder the New Testament warns us again and again, "Do not quench the Spirit" (1 Thessalonians 5:19) and "Do not grieve the Holy Spirit" (Ephesians 4:30).

But the story of Samson also teaches us that our God is a God of second chances. Samson would never have his eyes again. He would never have his freedom again. But his story isn't finished yet. As Judges 16:22 tells us, "the hair of his head began to grow again after it had been shaved." Though Samson had broken this final vow and had foolishly allowed his hair to be cut, God was giving Samson a second chance to keep his vow. Imprisoned and blind, forced to work like a beast of burden, like an ox that turned the grinding wheel, his hair began to grow back.

Throughout Samson's life, God had been watching over him, grieving over Samson's sin, grieving over the choices Samson made and the consequences he brought upon himself. And the consequences Samson brought upon himself through his sin were as natural and predictable as the laws of physics. You can no more defy the consequences of sin than you can repeal the law of gravity. If we persist in our rebellion, God lets us experience the consequences of that rebellion.

Samson learned this lesson through the harsh teacher of bitter experience. But he did learn a lesson. Verse 22 begins with one all-important word: "But…" That one word is the fulcrum, the tipping point of the entire story of Samson. Prior to that one word, Samson was a shallow, self-willed, spiritually insensitive man. But the Samson we meet after the word *but* is a changed man, a new creature. His life has turned a corner and now moves in a new direction.

Eyeless and enslaved in Gaza, Samson is down but not out. He has failed, but he is not forsaken. He has been humbled but not crushed. He was shorn of his hair and his power, but his hair is growing once more.

And God's power now rests on him again.

The Death and Redemption of Samson

Here is the conclusion of Samson story—and it is a conclusion both tragic and heroic, a story of death and redemption:

> Now the lords of the Philistines gathered to offer a great sacrifice to Dagon their god and to rejoice, and they said, "Our god has given Samson our enemy into our hand." And when the people saw him, they praised their god. For they said, "Our god has given our enemy into our hand, the ravager of our country, who has killed many of us." And when their hearts were merry, they said, "Call Samson, that he may entertain us." So they called Samson out of the prison, and he entertained them. They made him stand between the pillars. And Samson said to the young man who held him by the hand, "Let me feel the pillars on which the house rests, that I may lean

against them." Now the house was full of men and women. All the lords of the Philistines were there, and on the roof there were about 3,000 men and women, who looked on while Samson entertained.

Then Samson called to the LORD and said, "O LORD GOD, please remember me and please strengthen me only this once, O God, that I may be avenged on the Philistines for my two eyes." And Samson grasped the two middle pillars on which the house rested, and he leaned his weight against them, his right hand on the one and his left hand on the other. And Samson said, "Let me die with the Philistines." Then he bowed with all his strength, and the house fell upon the lords and upon all the people who were in it. So the dead whom he killed at his death were more than those whom he had killed during his life. Then his brothers and all his family came down and took him and brought him up and buried him between Zorah and Eshtaol in the tomb of Manoah his father. He had judged Israel twenty years (Judges 16:23-31).

The Philistines lived in a coastal region and served Dagon, one of their pagan gods. When the Philistines defeated Samson, they believed that Samson's God, Yahweh, had been defeated as well, and they gave Dagon the glory for that defeat. All the lords of the Philistines, their cult priests and warrior chieftains, then gathered to celebrate their victory over Samson and, in their minds, Dagon's victory over Yahweh. And they summoned Samson to serve as their entertainment.

Put yourself in Samson's place: You're blind and surrounded by three thousand enemies who mock you and taunt you while glorifying their demon god. You know you have brought suffering upon yourself, shame upon your nation, and dishonor upon the name of God. All these horrible consequences could have been avoided by simply obeying God and keeping your Nazirite vows. You, and only you, are responsible for handing this victory to your enemies.

How Samson must have berated himself for his foolishness and disobedience. Yet, though he had been unfaithful to God throughout his life, he was still a man of faith and he was faithful at the end. He prayed for the physical strength to punish and destroy his enemies—and he prayed, "Let me die with the Philistines."

When the Philistines had become sufficiently drunk, they began to drag the Lord's name through the mud. But God will not be mocked. The time had come for the Spirit of God to pour out his power upon Samson one last time.

Samson pushed with all his God-given strength against the weight-bearing pillars of the pagan temple, and the entire structure collapsed, killing all the Philistines at the celebration. In all his twenty years as judge over Israel, this was Samson's finest moment. It was the moment of his greatest spiritual strength as well as his greatest physical strength. He had come to the end of his own resources and had finally learned to depend on Yahweh alone. No longer would he use God's strength for his own selfish purposes. He trusted in the blessings of God himself.

After his eyes were taken from him, Samson no longer did what was right in his own eyes. From then on, he "saw" through eyes of faith. And God honored Samson's prayer of faith. God is always faithful to his promises, even when we break our vows. Samson brought more glory to God through his death than through his life.

In 2010, archaeologists announced the discovery of a temple at the site of the ancient Philistine city of Gath, in Israel's Tel Tzafit National Park. They discovered two cylindrical foundations where a pair of central pillars once supported the weight of the entire temple. One of the archaeologists, Professor Aren Maeir of Bar-Ilan University, said, "We're not saying this is the same temple where the story of Samson occurred…But this gives us a good idea of what image whoever wrote the story would have had of a Philistine temple."[36] In other words, this finding confirms that ancient Philistine temples were constructed just as the book of Judges describes.

If you visit Israel, you can take the Jerusalem-Tel Aviv highway to the Eshtaol Forest and climb to the top of a mountain that overlooks the city of Beit Shemesh, west of Jerusalem. On top of that mountain, with a panoramic view of the Judean Mountains, is a double tomb made of cut white stone topped by sky-blue domes. According to tradition, that double tomb is the final resting place of Samson and his father Manoah.

Delivered from the Dungeon

In 1948, Billy Graham was an evangelist for Youth for Christ International and president of Northwestern Bible College. He was aware that several preachers and evangelists had recently been accused of fraud, corruption, and immorality and that the reputation of the gospel had been tarnished by these scandals. So Billy Graham met with associate evangelist Grady Wilson, singer George Beverly Shea, and music director Cliff Barrows to fast and pray for God's direction. They met at the Barrows family farm near Modesto, California.

During that retreat, these men made a commitment to each

other. They would hold each other accountable for keeping their evangelistic organization honest and above reproach. The ministry's finances and attendance records would be an open book. They would promote unity with other Christian ministries and churches. And each man in the organization would live morally and faithfully before God. Billy Graham made a commitment that he would never travel or dine alone, nor would he even enter an elevator, with a woman who was not his wife.

The agreement these men made came to be known as "The Modesto Manifesto." And while the enemies of the gospel have repeatedly tried to find fault with Billy Graham and his organization, in more than six decades of ministry there has never been a hint of financial, ethical, or moral scandal around Dr. Graham and his ministry.

People of faith must also be found faithful. We all need a "Modesto Manifesto" of our own. The life of Samson serves as a warning for us all—and for the next generation. It's a warning against flirting with sin and compromising God's Word.

If you feel stripped of your strength, it's time to examine yourself. Perhaps it's time to come to the end of yourself and rely completely on God and his strength. He wants to lift you out of the prison you have made for yourself. He wants to take you out of the darkness and restore your sight.

It's a pattern we see again and again in Scripture. Peter sank to the depths of denying his Lord three times so that he might be delivered from boasting of his own abilities. The persecutor Saul had to be blinded and humbled in the dust of the Damascus Road so that God might raise him up as the mighty apostle to the Gentiles. And Samson, the judge and deliver of Israel, had to be humbled and robbed of his strength and his sight before God could use him in a significant way.

Lean on God for his strength. Let God's vision be your eyes. Let his will be your victory. Let go of your habitual sins, repent of your compromise, and let God deliver you from your dungeon in Gaza.

Conclusion

Doing What's Right
in God's Eyes

The book of Judges, of course, does not end with the death of Samson. The rest of the book reveals Israel's ever-increasing apostasy, immorality, and idolatry. Judges 17 and 18 tells the sordid story about Micah's pagan idol and its theft by some members of the tribe of Dan, and Judges 19 through 21 describes the near annihilation of the tribe of Benjamin, a battle sparked by the gruesome abuse and murder of a Levite's concubine.

Neither of these sections tells the story of a particular judge. Instead, they show the depths of depravity to which Israel has sunk through disobedience to God's commandments. The people of Israel have fallen to such a spiritual and moral low point that they see no problem whatsoever in worshiping the Lord and pagan idols side by side. This is the spiritual blindness that sets in when we neglect God's commandments.

The book of Judges concludes, once again, with this stinging indictment: "In those days there was no king in Israel. Everyone did what was right in his own eyes" (21:25). Joshua had told the people of Israel that God alone was to be their king. But Israel abandoned God and had no king. They did as they pleased. They followed their worst instincts and lusts. They worshiped false gods. They raped and murdered one another.

These were troubled times for God's people. Moral relativism permeated the culture of Israel, and the notion of moral absolutes was treated with ridicule and derision. Sexual immorality and perversion were not only tolerated but commended.

In short, life in that society was not so different from life in our own postmodern, post-Christian, anything-goes society. Our culture has been heavily Canaanized, and all around us, even in the church, everyone does what is right in their own eyes.

The Israelites in the time of the Judges expected God to bless them whether they obeyed him or not. In their spiritual immaturity, they felt entitled to God's blessings. But God's message to the people of Israel, which he repeatedly explained to them through the law and the prophets, was, "You cannot receive blessings from Yahweh while you live in disobedience. You can't have it both ways."

These days, people avoid words like *sin* or *disobedience*. They prefer to say "everybody does it" or "the old rules don't apply anymore" or "times have changed." It's true that times have changed, and not for the better. But God hasn't changed. He still says to us, "You cannot receive blessings from me while you live in disobedience. You can't have it both ways."

If you think you can be a discerning believer without spending time with God—think again. If you think you can be a woman of

God or a man of God without studying his Word—think again. If you think you can be super-spiritual without being a super-servant—think again. If you think you can substitute fame and reputation for character and integrity—think again. If you think you can use God's church or God's people to achieve your selfish goals—think again. If you think you can experience God's blessings without living in faithful obedience to him—think again.

I once heard the story of an American mother whose husband abandoned her and her daughter. The daughter became rebellious and spiteful. Finally, after one horrible argument, the daughter walked out. Weeks passed, and the daughter didn't come home and didn't even write or call. The mother was beside herself with worry and dread. She called all of her daughter's friends, but they either would not or could not tell her where her daughter was.

Months passed. Finally, a family friend called and gave the mother word that her daughter was living in London as a prostitute. The mother had no money for a plane ticket, so she sold everything she had, bought a ticket, and flew to London.

After she arrived there, she went from bar to bar with her daughter's picture, asking, "Have you seen this girl?" Finally, one bartender looked at the picture and said, "Yes, she comes here occasionally."

The mother posted her daughter's picture on the wall with the following message: "Please come home."

A few days later, the daughter came into the bar to pick up customers—and she saw her picture on the wall and read the message. Shaking and stammering, she asked the bartender, "Who put up that picture? Where did it come from?"

"There was a lady in here looking for you," he said. "She said she was your mother."

At that moment, the daughter realized how far she had wandered from the love of her mother. Sobbing, she took the picture down from the wall, and she went home to the one who loved her.

If you find yourself caught in the downward spiral of disobedience, if you are doing what is right in your own eyes rather than in God's, it's time to come home. The One who loves you is waiting.

Notes

1. Nicholas Humphrey, "What Shall We Tell the Children?," Amnesty Lecture, Oxford, February 21, 1997, www.edge.org/3rd_culture/humphrey/amnesty.html; excerpted in a slightly different form by Richard Dawkins, *The God Delusion* (New York: Houghton Mifflin, 2006), 326.

2. Peter Hitchens, *The Rage Against God* (Grand Rapids: Zondervan, 2010), 86-87.

3. Orlando Figes, *The Whisperers: Private Life in Stalin's Russia* (New York: Henry Holt, 2007), 20.

4. David Kupelian, "How Atheism Is Being Sold to America," *World Net Daily*, October 11, 2007, www.wnd.com/2007/10/43734/.

5. John Adams, letter to Thomas Jefferson, April 19, 1817, quoted by Paul F. Boller Jr. and John George Jr., *They Never Said It: A Book of Fake Quotes, Misquotes, and Misleading Attributions* (New York: Oxford University Press, 1989), 3.

6. Dennis P. Hollinger, "Is Jesus Really the Only Way to God," Gordon-Conwell Theological Seminary, *Contact Magazine*, Winter 2009, www.gordonconwell.edu/resources/Is-Jesus-Really-the-Only-Way-to-God.cfm.

7. I have more to say about spiritual warfare in my book, *Conquer: Your Battle Plan for Spiritual Victory* (Eugene, OR: Harvest House Publishers, 2015).

8. Archbishop of Canterbury Rowan Williams, "The Nature of Human Beings and the Question of Their Ultimate Origin," debate with Prof. Richard Dawkins, moderated by Sir Anthony Kenny, Sheldonian Theatre, Oxford, February 23, 2012, transcribed by the author from video at http://podcasts.ox.ac.uk/nature-human-beings-and-question-their-ultimate-origin-video.

9. William Provine, "Evolution Quotes," Bevets.com, http://bevets.com/equotesp5.htm.

10. William Provine, "Darwinism: Science or Naturalistic Philosophy?," debate between William B. Provine and Phillip E. Johnson at Stanford University, April 30, 1994, Access Research Network, volume 16, number 1, June 2, 1995, www.arn.org/docs/orpages/or161/161main.htm.

11. F. Scott Fitzgerald, *Echoes of the Jazz Age* (New York: New Directions Publishing, 1931), xvi.

12. Mark Braun, "The Quiet Church in the Roaring Twenties," WELS *Forward in Christ*, Wisconsin Evangelical Lutheran Synod, July 2000, www.wels.net/news-events/forward-in-christ/july-2000/quiet-church-in-roaring-twenties?page=0,1.

13. Robert Rector, "Marriage: America's Greatest Weapon Against Child Poverty," Heritage Foundation, September 5, 2012, www.heritage.org/research/reports/2012/09/marriage-americas-greatest-weapon-against-child-poverty.

14. The Week Staff, "The Internet Porn 'Epidemic': By the Numbers," *The Week*, June 17, 2010, http://theweek.com/article/index/204156/the-internet-porn-epidemic-by-the-numbers.

15. Mark McHugh, "The Cost of Kidding Yourself," Across the Streetnet, November 28, 2012, http://acrossthestreet.wordpress.com/2012/11/28/the-cost-of-kidding-yourself/.

16. Federal Reserve Bank of St. Louis, Economic Research, "Employment—Population Ratio—Men (LNS12300001)," February 1, 2013, http://research.stlouisfed.org/fred2/series/LNS12300001.

17. United States Department of Agriculture, Supplemental Nutrition Assistance Program, data as of February 8, 2013, www.fns.usda.gov/pd/34snapmonthly.htm.

18. United States Treasury, TreasuryDirect, "The Debt to the Penny and Who Holds It," March 5, 2013, www.treasurydirect.gov/NP/BPDLogin?application=np.

19. Mamta Badkar, "13 Huge Trends in America's Prescription Drug Habit," *Business Insider*, December 2010, www.businessinsider.com/trends-prescription-drug-use-2011-4#spending-on-medication-was-60-billion-higher-than-five-years-ago-1.

20. Al Gore, *Earth in the Balance* (New York: Penguin, 1993), 258-59.

21. Ibid., 259.

22. Ibid., 260.

23. Matthew Sleeth, *Hope for Humanity, Part 2: Guidebook* (Grand Rapids: Zondervan, 2010), 71.

24. John S. Dickerson, "The Decline of Evangelical America," *New York Times*, December 15, 2012, www.nytimes.com/2012/12/16/opinion/sunday/the-decline-of-evangelical-america.html?pagewanted=all&_r=0.

25. Malcolm Muggeridge, *The End of Christendom* (Grand Rapids: Eerdmans, 1980), 21.

26. Mike Howerton, *Glorious Mess: Encountering God's Relentless Grace for Imperfect People* (Grand Rapids: Baker Books, 2012), 142.

27. Susan Pellowe, "Susanna Wesley's Biography," SusanPellowe.com, http://susanpellowe.com/susanna-wesley.htm.

28. Josh McDowell, *True or False: Workbook Leader's Guide* (Wheaton, IL: Tyndale, 2003), 6.

29. R.A. Torrey, *Torrey on Prayer* (Alachua, FL: Bridge-Logos, 2009), 160.

30. James Kittelson, *Luther the Reformer* (Minneapolis: Augsburg Fortress, 1986), 79.

31. Quoted in Charles R. Swindoll, *Growing Strong in the Seasons of Life* (Grand Rapids: Zondervan, 1983), 385.

32. Jonathan MacLeod, "Don't Judge Others...Judge Yourself!," SermonCentral.com, May 2001, www.sermoncentral.com/sermons/dont-judge-others----judge-yourself-jonathan-mcleod-sermon-on-christian-values-38016.asp?page=2.

33. David Treybig, "If Children Could Choose Their Parents," *Good News*, July–August 1998, www.ucg.org/marriage-and-family/if-children-could-choose-their-parents/.

34. Richard J. Krejcir, "Statistics on Pastors," *Into Thy Word*, 2007, www.intothyword.org/apps/articles/?articleid=36562.

35. Warren W. Wiersbe, *The Wiersbe Bible Commentary: Old Testament* (Colorado Springs: David C. Cook, 2007), 421.

36. Ben Hartman, "Temple Found in Philistine Home of Goliath," *Jerusalem Post*, July 29, 2010, www.jpost.com/Features/InThespotlight/Article.aspx?id=182962.

About Michael Youssef

Michael Youssef was born in Egypt and lived in Lebanon and Australia before coming to the United States. He has degrees from Australia and the US, and he earned a PhD in social anthropology from Emory University. Michael served for nearly ten years with the Haggai Institute, traveling around the world teaching leadership principles. He rose to the position of managing director at the age of thirty-one, and the family settled in Atlanta.

Dr. Youssef founded The Church of The Apostles in 1987 with fewer than forty adults with the mission to "equip the saints and seek the lost." The church has since grown to a congregation of over three thousand. This church on a hill was the launching pad for Leading The Way, an international ministry whose radio and television programs are heard by millions at home and abroad.

For more on Michael Youssef, The Church of The Apostles, and Leading The Way, visit apostles.org and www.leadingtheway.org.

Conquer

Your Battle Plan for Spiritual Victory

Devil. Great deceiver. Evil one. Father of lies. Satan.

Many names. One enemy. And whether you realize it or not, you are on a spiritual battlefield with this enemy every day. How do you prepare to defend yourself?

In *Conquer*, Michael Youssef says you first need to know everything you can about your enemy. What are Satan's strengths? What are his weaknesses? How does he like to attack? When is he most likely to attack? Are there areas of your life where you are vulnerable and he seems to control the battlefield?

Only when you know your enemy inside and out can you plan and carry out a specific counterattack to defeat him. The final victory will be Christ's, of course. That's a promise from God. But as a Christian, you can actively take part in resisting the devil…and watching him flee.

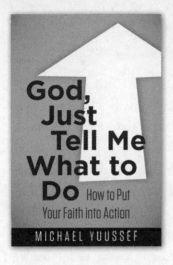

God, Just Tell Me What to Do
How to Put Your Faith into Action

God is constantly teaching us through our daily experiences. He wants us to master today's challenges and to be equipped to take on even greater challenges tomorrow. He wants our lives to reveal the reality of our growing faith and godly character.

In *God, Just Tell Me What to Do,* Michael Youssef offers biblical wisdom and encouragement to help you live out your Christian faith in such important areas as

- using your resources wisely
- thriving through trials and temptations
- understanding and obeying the Word of God
- guarding against the pressures of culture
- taming your tongue

As you learn to put your faith into action as a follower of Christ, you will discover depths of strength, courage, and joy you never knew were waiting for you.

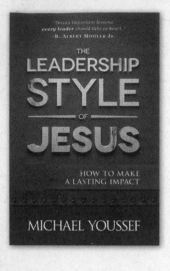

The Leadership Style of Jesus
How to Make a Lasting Impact

No matter what leadership arena you serve in—whether leading a family, a church, a civic organization, a company—adopting the leadership example of Jesus will make you more effective and productive. Leadership is influence, and no leader has had greater influence on the world than Jesus Christ. The lessons of His leadership style are practical, learnable skills that you can apply today.

Michael Youssef, who has executive experience in worldwide ministries, has examined the leadership Jesus modeled and suggests Christlike qualities every leader needs. But he doesn't stop there. With Jesus as the standard, Dr. Youssef considers how to deal with the temptations and pressures leaders face, including ego, anger, loneliness, criticism, the use of power, and passing the torch to others.

If you are in search of excellence in developing your leadership abilities, you will find much to aid your quest in this close-up look at Jesus—the greatest leader who ever lived.

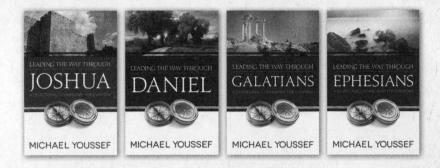

Leading the Way Through the Bible
Commentary Series

About the Series: The Leading the Way Through the Bible commentary series will not only increase your Bible knowledge, but it will motivate you to apply God's Word to the problems of our hurting world and to a deeper and more obedient walk with Jesus Christ. The writing is lively, informal, and packed with stories that illustrate the truth of God's Word. The Leading the Way series is a call to action—and a call to the exciting adventure of living for Christ.

Books in this series:

Leading the Way Through Joshua
Leading the Way Through Daniel
Leading the Way Through Galatians
Leading the Way Through Ephesians

To learn more about Harvest House books and
to read sample chapters, visit our website:

www.harvesthousepublishers.com

HARVEST HOUSE PUBLISHERS
EUGENE, OREGON